Tranter's Terrain

Tranter's Terrain

*by Michael and
Alison Pritchard*

Neil Wilson Publishing Ltd • Glasgow

© Michael and Alison Pritchard 1994
Published by Neil Wilson Publishing Ltd
309 The Pentagon Centre
36 Washington Street
GLASGOW G3 8AZ

Tel: 041-221-1117
Fax: 041-221-5363

A catalogue record for this book is available from the British Library.
ISBN 1-897784-23-6

Typeset in 11/13pt Garamond by Face to Face Design Services, Glasgow

Printed in Musselburgh by Scotprint Ltd

Contents

CENTRAL SCOTLAND

SOUTHERN SCOTLAND

Borders Region

Foreword

I congratulate Michael and Alison Pritchard on their devoted and admirable labours, as demonstrated in the following pages of this most useful book. Not only much reading of my frequently inadequate efforts to portray Scotland's story has clearly been entailed, but also a great deal of relevant research, a vast amount of travel, visiting and ferreting-out — all demanding considerable patience, dedication and judgement as well as enthusiasm. They have obviously had to traverse the length and breadth of the land in their endeavours, and that in itself is no light undertaking, as I know well, although rewarding also.

I hope that their efforts may prove of interest and value to many, and not only to those who are readers of my novels; for here, in brief and easily-read form is a work of much worth to all who care for and concern themselves with our colourful and dramatic homeland and its equally colourful story.

Here is a means of not only entering more fully into the novels themselves, but of discovering and knowing the land and countryside better in general — and, yes, even if you do not all actually leave your own firesides to do it!

My salutations to all concerned.

Nigel Tranter
Aberlady

Introduction

It all began with a friend's question — 'I am reading a Nigel Tranter book. Is there really such a place as Fast Castle? I can't find it on the map!' As it happens we could answer the query without any trouble — 'Of course it's a real place, as are, or were, all of the places in the Tranter books. We'll get a map and show you where!'

The realisation came later that many readers of the Tranter novels did not know that the places referred to are all real and historical locations. The vivid, visual, writing creates in the mind's eye the scenes and settings that turn the reader into an explorer of a thousand years of living history. For a small nation Scotland has an all-action story which is set against a backdrop of unequalled diversity. As it unfolds it leads the reader across the length and breadth of the land. During the past forty years of walking and driving the byways and highways of Scotland, we have visited a great many of the places named in the books. Often, without realising the part they had played in history, they would merely be noted in the passing, then later while reading a passage in the latest Tranter novel the scene would come to life, for we had been there and in our imagination we could see it as it really was.

So this guide was born, not only to help others who want to find out quickly a little bit about the places and people as they read his books, but also to go with Nigel Tranter and explore Scotland as it was hundreds of years ago. This simple guide will answer at least some of the questions that often arise: Does it still exist? Where is such and such a place? Has it changed out of all recognition?

It would need a library to answer all the questions, not just one guide book, so here we have set out to provide as many answers as we can. The places chosen are a cross section from all the books and often appear in many of them. We indicate where to find the towns, villages, castles and settings. Enough background information is given to provide a starting point but not too much, for this is essentially a guide for explorers.

With this book Tranter fans, Scots or visitors alike, can set out time and time again on journeys of exploration that will take them to both well known and little-known places alike. The armchair explorer can similarly settle back with book and maps in comfort to travel in the mind where he or she will. And for those who have not yet read the novels of Nigel Tranter, then this book really will prove invaluable.

We would like to express our grateful thanks to Nigel Tranter for his very generous help and encouragement during the preparation of this guide. Nigel has truly opened up all of Scotland to our own personal exploration through his books and we have greatly enjoyed the very many hours of enjoyment the reading of his novels have given us.

To Rona — we must say thanks for asking that one question which started us off on this project, although we had no idea what we were letting ourselves in for!

Welcome to Tranter's Terrain...the historical canvas of Scotland on which Nigel Tranter has painted his creations for some 50 years.

Michael & Alison Pritchard
Fowlis Wester
January 1994

How to use this guide

To use this guide to its full advantage, Tranter's Terrain explorers will find that each entry has:

The entry name

The entry code

OS Grid Reference Number (OS Landranger Series required)

Nearest Town or Village

Entries marked ⚜ are not normally open or accessible to the public

The entries have been allocated to three main geographical areas: Highland (H) – north of the 'Highland line' which we have defined as an imaginary boundary running from west to east from the Firth of Clyde, through Loch Long, thence to Ardlui on Loch Lomond. From there it goes east-north-east via Ballinluig in Perthshire to St Cyrus on the coast above Montrose. Central (C) – is the area south of the Highland line to the Forth and Clyde valleys. South (S) is the area below the Forth and Clyde including the English side of the Border. The entries are listed by local government regions and the maps show the location of each entry which is identified alphabetically and given its area precursor (H, C or S) followed by an ascending numeral. For instance Threave Castle (the cover photograph) will be found under Southern Scotland (Dumfries and Galloway region), reference S70 on page 99.

Once you have located the place in which you are interested, use your own road maps to identify the nearest town or village, then the actual site. For those who use Ordnance Survey maps or road atlases the grid number is given. This will, of course, take you directly to the location square you require. The maps in this book act merely as guides and you should always refer to larger scale maps for accuracy.

Historical titles by Nigel Tranter

The Queen's Grace (1953)
MacGregor's Gathering (1957)
Balefire (1958)
The Clansman (1959)
Lord and Master (1961)
Gold for Prince Charlie (1962)
The Courtesan (1963)
Chain of Destiny (1964)
Past Master (1965)
Stake in the Kingdom (1966)
Lion Let Loose (1967)
Black Douglas (1968)
The Steps to the Empty Throne (1969)
The Path of the Hero King (1970)
Young Montrose (1972)
Montrose: The Captain-General (1973)
The Wisest Fool (1974)
The Wallace (1975)
Lords of Misrule (1976)
A Folly of Princes (1977)
The Captive Crown (1977)
Macbeth the King (1978)

Margaret the Queen (1979)
David the Prince (1980)
True Thomas (1981)
The Patriot (1982)
Lord of the Isles (1983)
Unicorn Rampant (1984)
The Riven Realm (1984)
James By the Grace of God (1985)
Rough Wooing (1986)
Columba (1987)
Flowers of Chivalry (1988)
Mail Royal (1989)
Warden of the Queen's March (1989)
Kenneth (1990)
Crusader (1991)
The Price of the King's Peace (1991)
Children of the Mist (1992)
Druid Sacrifice (1993)
Tapestry of the Boar (1993)

All books listed were published by Hodder & Stoughton

Bibliography

Portrait of Mull, Portrait of Iona; Robert Hale,1987
Islands series; David & Charles
Murray Handbook of Scotland 1894; David & Charles, 1971
Robert the Bruce, GWS Barrow; EUP, 1988
Bannockburn, WM Mackenzie; James Maclehose & Sons, 1913
Historic Scenes in Perthshire, W Marshall; Oliphant, Anderson & Ferrier, 1881
Forteviot, Neil Meldrum; Alexander Gardener, 1926
Shell Guide to Scotland, Moray McLaren; Ebury Press, 1965
Charles Edward Stuart, David Daiches; Thames & Hudson, 1973
The Survival of Scotland, Eric Linklater; Heinemann, 1968
In Scotland Again, HV Morton; Methuen & Co, 1933
The Road to Rannoch & The Isles, Ratcliffe Barnett; John Grant Ltd, 1946
Castles of Scotland, Ian Grimble; BBC Books, 1987
The Fortified House in Scotland, Nigel Tranter; Mercat Press, 1986
History of Dundee 1878; Winter, Duncan & Co, 1878
The Making of a King, Caroline Bingham; Wm Collins, 1968
Edinburgh, John Fulleylove & Rosaline Masson; Adam & Ch Black, 1912
Norham Castle, CH Hunter Blair & HL Honeyman; HMSO, 1966
Wooler, Ford, Chillingham and the Cheviots, Frank Graham; Frank Graham, 1976
Bowmen of England, Donald Featherstone; Jarrolds Ltd, 1967
Glen Trool, Editor: HL Edlin; HMSO, 1965
Imperial Gazetteer of Scotland 1864; A Fullarton & Co, 1864
Scotland – A New History, Michael Lynch; Century Ltd, 1991
Grampian Battlefields, Peter Marner; AUP, 1990

Other historical titles published by NWP

The Story of Scotland
Nigel Tranter
ISBN   1-897784-07-4 £6.99 Pbk

Tales and Traditions of Scottish Castles
Nigel Tranter
ISBN   1-897784-13-9 £5.99 Pbk

On A Scotch Bard
An illustrated life of Robert Burns
Keith Mitchell
ISBN   1-897784-22-8 £4.99 Pbk

The Hogmanay Companion
Hugh Douglas
ISBN   1-897784-12-0 £5.99 Pbk

Capital Walks in Edinburgh — The New Town
David Dick
ISBN   1-897784-20-1 £5.99 Pbk

Chronology

AD 84	The Battle of Mons Graupius
409	The Roman Army leaves Britain
563	St Columba arrives in Iona from Ireland
800	The Norwegians start to raid, settle the north and west
843	Kenneth MacAlpin of Dalriada defeats the Picts. Capital in Forteviot
937	Athelstan defeats league of Scots, British and Norsemen at Brunanburgh
940-946	Edmund conquers Strathclyde and gives it in fief to Malcolm I
1016	Malcolm II defeats Northumbrians at Carham
1018	Malcolm II defeats the Angles at Carham on the Tweed
1034	Malcolm II's grandson, Duncan I becomes King of Scotland
1040-57	Macbeth
1057	Duncan I's son, Malcolm Canmore, kills Macbeth
1057-58	Lulach, stepson of Macbeth, succeeds to throne
1058	Malcolm Canmore kills Lulach; succeeds as Malcolm III, King of Scots
1070	Malcolm III marries Margaret, daughter of Edward the Confessor. English influence increases
1072	William the Conqueror invades Scotland and makes Malcolm III (Canmore) pay homage at Abernethy. Malcolm moves the capital to Edinburgh
1093-94	Donald Bane
1094	Duncan II overthrows Donald Bane but dies before end of the year

1094-97	Donald Bane returns to the throne
1097-1107	Edgar, third son of Margaret, reigns
1107-24	Alexander I, fifth son of Margaret
1124	David I grants estates to Anglo-Normans
1153-65	Malcolm IV
1164	Somerled, Lord of the Isles, killed
1165-1214	William the Lion
1174	William signs the Treaty of Falaise, subjecting Scotland to England
1188	Richard I sells back Scottish independence
1214-49	Alexander II
1249	Alexander III succeeds to throne
1263	Alexander III defeats Norsemen at Largs
1286	Alexander III dies and succession crisis ensues
1290	Margaret, the Maid of Norway, dies on voyage to Scotland
1290-92	First interregnum: Edward I of England claims throne
1291	Edward I asked to adjudicate — selects John de Balliol in preference to Robert de Bruce
1295	John de Balliol revolts against Edward I
1296	Balliol refuses Edward I's demands, declares Scotland to be his fiefdom; Ragman's Roll
1297	William Wallace starts the rebellion against English rule and defeats the English at Stirling Bridge
1298	Edward I defeats Wallace at Falkirk
1303	Wallace captures Stirling
1305	Wallace executed
1306	Robert the Bruce is crowned and later defeated at Methven
1307-10	Robert I wins Battle of Loudoun. Death of Edward I
1314	Robert the Bruce defeats the English at Battle of Bannockburn
1320	Declaration of Arbroath
1328	Treaty of Northampton

1332	Earl of Mar defeated at Dupplin
1333	Battle of Halidon Hill — Scots defeated
1346	Battle of Neville's Cross. Scots invade England — David II captured
1358	David II released
1371	Robert II becomes first Stewart King
1388	Battle of Otterburn
1390-1403	Robert III
1406	The future James I captured
1411	Battle of Harlaw
1424	James I returns to Scotland
1437	James I killed
1437-60	James II — internal warfare between the Crown and Earls of Douglas
1460	James II killed by cannon exploding at Roxburgh Castle
1488	James III killed after the Battle of Sauchieburn
1513	James IV killed at Battle of Flodden
1523	The Borders are harried by the English
1535	The Border Lairds are instructed to fortify their houses
1542	James V dies
1544	The Rough Wooing
1547	The Scots defeated at the Battle of Pinkie
1548	Mary Queen of Scots is sent to France
1557	The Lords of the Congregation sign the First Covenant
1558	Elizabeth I becomes Queen of England
1559	Mary Queen of Scots's husband, Francois II, becomes King of France
1560	French troops besieged in Leith The Regent Marie of Guise dies
1561	Mary Stuart, Queen of Scots, returns to Scotland
1562	Battle of Corrochie
1565	Mary marries Henry Lord Darnley
1567	Darnley is murdered. Bothwell marries the Queen.

	At Carberry Hill Bothwell goes into exile and the Queen is held prisoner at Loch Leven Castle. Mary is forced to abdicate in favour of her son James
1568	Mary escapes from Loch Leven, is defeated at Langside and flees to England to be held prisoner by Elizabeth I
1573	Edinburgh Castle, held for Queen Mary finally surrendered
1587	Mary Queen of Scots executed at Fotheringay
1594	Battle of Glenlivet
1603	Elizabeth I dies
1603	James VI of Scotland crowned as James I of England
1624	Baronetcies of Nova Scotia
1633	Charles I crowned King of Scotland at Scone
1638	The signing of the National Covenant
1642	Outbreak of Civil War in England
1645	Montrose raises an army for Charles I and is defeated at Philiphaugh
1650	Montrose returns and is executed by Marquis of Argyll
1660	The Restoration of Charles II
1679	Battle of Bothwell Brig
1688	The Glorious Revolution. William of Orange deposes James VII and II, whose army is led by Graham of Claverhouse (Bonnie Dundee), killed at the Battle of Killiecrankie
1692	The massacre of Glencoe
1695	The Darien Scheme
1707	The Treaty of Union
1714	George I of Hanover
1715	Jacobite Rising — Battle of Sheriffmuir
1719	Jacobite Rising — Battle of Glenshiel
1745	Jacobite Rising under Prince Charles Edward
1746	Battle of Culloden

THE HIGHLANDS

TYNDRUM   H60

NN3429

About one mile south of the village is Dail Righ where tradition
states that the battle between Robert the Bruce and Macdougall
of Lorn took place in 1306. Having been crowned, and then
defeated at Methven, the Bruce headed west with only a small
force including his Queen, daughter and a few others. Ambushed
by the Macdougalls in the narrow pass, the women were sent
north while Bruce fought off the attackers. During the struggle
the King's brooch was lost and after the battle found by the
MacDougalls. It was then taken to Dunollie Castle and became
known as the Brooch of Lorn.

ABERDEEN H1
NJ9206

> *'It is the King's cause that I am concerned with,*
> *Aberdeen is a large city. We cannot garrison it, or*
> *hold it.'*
> MONTROSE IN THE CAPTAIN GENERAL

Europe's oil capital hides behind the facade of historic Aberdeen. In exploring the city, use the street names to locate the scenes of the past. The Bridge of Dee remains, asa do Castle Street and Justice Mill Lane. St Machar's Cathedral in Old Aberdeen is an essential visit.

ALFORD   H3
NJ5716

To the west of the village will be found the battlefield of the same name where, on the 2nd July 1645, the Marquis of Montrose fought General Baillie in one of the bloodiest battles ever fought in the north-east of Scotland. Look for the Gordon Stone — it marks the spot where Lord George Gordon who commanded the horse on the right of Montrose's line, was killed.

BALVENIE CASTLE   H8
NJ3240   *Dufftown*

Now a ruin, Balvenie Castle is still an impressive example of a courtyard castle. One of the oldest stone castles in Scotland, it was successively a stronghold of the Comyns, the Douglases and the Stuarts. Standing above the River Fiddich, its entrance via a vaulted pend with iron yett will create the atmosphere of the turbulent past for today's explorer.

BANFF CASTLE   H9
NJ6864   *Banff*

Originally built to defend the coast from the Viking invasion, nothing now remains of the stronghold which was a royal palace. Malcolm IV is considered to have made this his residence in 1160 and a constable or thane resided there and passed sentence in the absence of the monarch. A Carmelite monastery was founded at the same time as the castle.

BRAEMAR CASTLE   H11
NO1592   *Braemar*

Tradition says that the first castle at Braemar was built upon a rock on the east side of the Clunie Water by Malcolm Canmore. The present castle dates from the early 1600s and is to the north of the town. The exterior of the castle today is that of the fortress rebuilt in 1778. The government reconstruction turned it into both barracks and fort, complete with star-shaped curtain wall.

CORGARFF CASTLE   H17
NJ2508   *Cock Bridge*
Believed to have been originally built by an Earl of Mar, Corgarff
was burned by the Gordons and so perished 27 people. The building dates from 1537 and was purchased by the government in
1746 and converted to a military barracks.

CULLEN CASTLE   H19
NJ5066   *Cullen*
The old castle has been remodelled over the years. Its interest to
the explorer is that close by was a building in which Robert the
Bruce's wife Elizabeth died in 1327.

DARNAWAY CASTLE   H21
NH9955   *Forres*

> *Since Moray had been packed off to his northern*
> *fastness at Darnaway, a certain aura of peace had*
> *descended upon the Court.*
> THE COURTESAN

The seat of the Earls of Moray, this imposing mansion is set in
the Findhorn Valley. The only remnant of the early castle built
around 1450 is the Hall which has been incorporated into the
Gothic-style house built in the early 1800 s. Queen Mary held
court here in 1664 and it later became a haunt of James IV who
gave it to his mistress, Lady Janet Kennedy.

DUNNOTTAR CASTLE   H26
NO8883   *Stonehaven*
The approach to the ruins of this magnificent castle is through a
ravine which shows the vast extent of the site, the scene of many
battles as far back as the Pictish period. Standing upon a steep
rock which projects into the North Sea, the castle was besieged
by Cromwell in 1651 and chosen as the strongest place in the

country to hide the regalia of Scotland during the Commonwealth of 1649-53.

ELGIN   H30
NJ2163

> *'They crossed the land swiftly. Inverness they burned.*
> *They turned south for Forres and Elgin, harrying,*
> *slaying.'*
>
> MARIOTA IN *A FOLLY OF PRINCES*

A thriving town in the Laigh of Moray, dominated by the ruins of Elgin Cathedral, known as the Lanthorn of the North. Built on the site of an old church by Bishop Andrew Moray in 1224, the original fabric was destroyed by fire in 1390 by Robert II's son, Alexander Stuart — The Wolf of Badenoch, and it took many years to rebuild. Extensive ruins of the cathedral and the adjoining chapter house remain. To the west of the cathedral on the summit of Lady Hill are fragments of the remains of Elgin castle which stood from the 12th century and at one time was occupied by Edward I of England.

The Cathedral of Elgin

FYVIE CASTLE   H34
NJ7639   *Fyvie*

A great castle and a battle bear the name Fyvie. Within a royal
forest, the original castle was built as an administrative centre in
the 13th century and granted to Sir Henry Preston in 1390. The
battle took place in 1644 between James Graham, Marquis of
Montrose – the King's Lieutenant and Archibald Campbell, Earl
of Argyll who commanded the Covenanter forces. Montrose won
the battle and held the ground, but when a couple of days later
Argyll finally withdrew, he too made off for Turriff.

GIGHT CASTLE   H35
NJ8239   *Fyvie*

In the Ythan valley, between Fyvie and Methlick, are the ruins of
Gight Castle, once the stronghold of the Gordons of Gight. A
monument on farmland at Lewes, near Fyvie marks the site of
the Priory of St Mary, thought to have been founded in the 12th
century by Fergus, Earl of Buchan.

HARLAW   H38
NJ7424   *Inverurie*

Red Harlaw was the most bloody battle ever fought in North-
east Scotland. In 1411 Donald, Lord of the Isles claimed the
Earldom of Ross and headed with his followers across Scotland
aiming to plunder Aberdeen. In his way stood Alexander, Earl of
Mar and those who thought otherwise. Alexander prevailed and
won the day. Look for the Harlaw Monument and battlefield
some three miles north of Inverurie.

HUNTLY CASTLE   H39
NJ5340   *Huntly*

Site of the great castle of Strathbogie, capital and power base of
the Gordons. The story of the development of such a castle is
there for all to see from the original Norman mote and medieval
keep, to the earthworks of the Civil War and the then great

palace of the first Marquess of Huntly. It was in the 18th century that the modern town of Huntly grew up to replace the old barony that clustered round the castle.

INVERURIE   H43
NJ7721

> *'My Lord Montrose — as Lieutenant-General, you will*
> *return to your force at Inverurie, to prosecute your*
> *campaign with all address. And with increased*
> *vigour.'*
> FIELD-MARSHAL LESLIE IN *THE YOUNG MONTROSE*

An ancient royal burgh at the junction of the Rivers Don and Ury, founded by the great-great-grandfather of Robert the Bruce, David of Huntingdon. An earth mound known as the Bass is the site of an old motte and bailey castle which was walled up by the citizens of Inverurie as the inhabitants were infected by the plague. Robert the Bruce is said to have lain gravely ill near Inverurie before his victory over the Comyns at the Battle of Barra.

KILDRUMMY CASTLE   H46
NJ4516   *Alford*
One of the most powerful strongholds in the north. It was to Kildrummy that Robert the Bruce sent his Queen and her ladies after the battle of Methven. Besieged, the Queen escaped but a traitor fired the castle. Later the castle was again besieged but successfully defended by Bruce's sister, Christian.

KINTORE   H48
NJ7816
Standing in what was the royal forest about 1 mile from the town of Kintore, are the ruins of Hallforest Castle. The castle was built in the early 14th century and used as a royal hunting lodge. Part of the forest was granted by Robert the Bruce to Sir Robert de Keith after Bannockburn in 1314.

MIDMAR CASTLE H52
NJ7005   *Echt*

A fine, attractive tower house standing on the slopes of the Hill of Fare, near to the village of Echt. Probably dating from the 16th century, the ownership has changed hands many times.

OLDMELDRUM H53
NJ8027

A small burgh whose place in history is assured by the nearby site of Bruce's Battle of Barra. Just to the south-west of the town and known today as 'the King's Field' is the place where the Bruce achieved a decisive victory over his Comyn enemies in 1307.

TURRIFF H59
NJ7149

Turriff's place in Scotland's history is assured. It is remembered for the fact that the first serious clash after the signing of the National Covenant occurred here in May 1639. The town itself has a long history going back to the 12th century.

ACHNACARRY CASTLE   H2
NN1787   *Spean Bridge*

The present castle, seat of the Camerons of Lochiel, is not the original which was destroyed in 1746. The old castle was on a site nearby.

ARDVRECK CASTLE   H4
NC2323   *Lochinver*

On a rocky peninsula that cuts into the waters of Loch Assynt are the ruined remains of the Macleod stronghold of Ardvreck Castle. It was here that the great Marquis of Montrose was captured and held prisoner after his defeat at Carbisdale in 1650.

AULDEARN
NH9155

H7
Nairn

> *'We have won victories, yes – but without this man*
> *we might well have won none. Auldearn, of which*
> *you have just heard the King praise, was almost*
> *wholly his victory.'*
> MONTROSE OF COLKITTO IN THE CAPTAIN GENERAL

A few miles to the east of Nairn, the village and battlefield of Auldearn mark one of the battles so brilliantly fought by the Marquis of Montrose against the forces of the covenanters commanded by General Hurry. The burial ground of Nairn contains the graves of covenanters who fell in the battle.

CARBISDALE
NH5795

H12
Bonar Bridge

> *'Carbisdale was over, not so much a battle as a*
> *protracted folly and disaster.'*
> MONTROSE IN THE CAPTAIN GENERAL

The site of the final battle and defeat of the great Marquis of Montrose. On 27th April 1650 at about 3pm, Colonel Archibald Strachan ambushed the Royalist force on the strath not far from the village of Culrain. Unable to beat off the strong cavalry force, the Royalist rebels were defeated. Montrose was captured three days later at Ardvreck Castle and went to meet the hangman at Edinburgh on 21st of May.

CASTLE GRANT
NJ0430

H13
Grantown-on-Spey

Originally built during the 15th and 16th centuries by the Grants and known as Freuchie, the name was changed later. The present castle, situated just outside the town of Grantown-on-Spey, is constituted mainly from the additions by John Adam in 1765. The castle is currently up for sale.

CASTLE MOIL   H14
NG7526   *Kyleakin*

The ruin of the castle sits on its rock overlooking Kyle of Lochalsh
as it has done since it was built by a Norse Princess, or so we are
told. The Princess, however, had a good eye for the main chance
and, as it is situated at the narrowest point of the kyle, she had a
giant chain stretched across the water and levied a toll on all who
would sail through.

CASTLE TIORAM   H16
NM6672   *Acharacle*

This impressive castle set on a rocky outcrop in the mouth of
Loch Moidart has a commanding appearance. The seat of
Clanranald, built during the 13th and 14th centuries with later
additions, it saw much turmoil and bloodshed over the years,
being attacked from both land and sea. The castle was occupied
by Cromwell as a garrison and finally, during the Jacobite Rising
of 1715, it was set ablaze by its owner to prevent it falling into
the hands of the government troops.

CORRYARRACK PASS   H18
NN4298   *Fort Augustus*

The pass and old military road from Badenoch to the Great
Glen. Well worth making the walk through it.

CULLODEN   H20
NH7445   *Inverness*

The open moor upon which the Jacobite cause and army of
Prince Charles Edward Stuart (the Young Pretender) was lost to
the government forces under the Duke of Cumberland in 1746.
The last major battle to be fought on British soil was only to last
some 40 minutes. Visit the graves of the clans, the old Leanach
Cottage, the Memorial Cairn and the National Trust for Scotland Centre to see the audio-visual presentation that brings to
life the final battle of the clan system under the House of Stuart

against the forces of repression and change under the House of Hanover.

DUNVEGAN CASTLE   H28
NG2449   *Dunvegan*

Fortress home of the Chiefs of Clan Macleod, it is within its walls that the world famous 'Fairy Flag' is kept secure. Built in the 13th century, the massive curtain wall provided the basis of the castle as it is today. Added to over the years, Dunvegan is still a hold of strength and power, for who would wish to be incarcerated in its dungeon? A violent and at times bloody past can be conjured up from the history of this stronghold of the Macleods.

FORT AUGUSTUS   H32
NH3709

The village here was originally known as Kilcumin, the site of the cell or church of Cumin, an early abbot of Iona. Of the fort itself, a little remains and can be found preserved in the north-west corner of the now closed Abbey School.

FORT WILLIAM   H33
NN1073

The town of Fort William was originally a village named Gordonsburgh, later changed to Maryburgh but by popular usage has changed to that of the garrison fort built on the site of an earlier wooden fort. Even the latter has now gone.

Glencoe – a wild and desolate place

GLENCOE
H36
NM1059
Fort William

One of the most famous glens in all Scotland – a wild and desolate place, it is the home of myths going back to the poems of Ossian who was traditionally said to have been born in a cave in Glencoe. The area abounds in tales of Fingal and the Gaelic heroes. On a rather more factual basis, the Massacre of the Macdonalds in 1692 has fed the Scots imagination for generations. Visit the site of the original village and Signal Rock whilst the really active should seek out the Hidden Valley. Take any hillwalking excursions very seriously; Glencoe does not suffer fools gladly.

GLENELG   H37
NG8119   *Shiel Bridge*
A tiny village close to the narrows of Kyle Rhea. The steep moun-
tain pass of Mam Rattachan and ferry across the fast flowing
waters make this the adventurous way to Skye. The waters here
would have seen the longships of the Norse and the Lords of the
Isles. Boswell and Johnson crossed to Skye this way.

INVERGARRY CASTLE   H41
NH3100   *Fort Augustus*
On the shores of Loch Oich are the ruins of Invergarry Castle,
the ancestral home and fortress of the Macdonells of Glengarry.
The castle was built and destroyed twice. It was garrisoned before
the Battle of Killiecrankie in 1689, but burned down. Once more
rebuilt, Prince Charles Edward Stuart visited it before and after
the Battle of Culloden but the Duke of Cumberland then destroyed the castle.

INVERLOCHY CASTLE   H42
NN1376   *Fort William*

*...that evening, feasting on Campbell provision once
more, in the Great Hall of Inverlochy castle, part-
derelict but a palace compared with their quarters of
recent nights, Montrose called together such of his
officers as were available...*
THE YOUNG MONTROSE

The castle of Inverlochy presents a mystery for the explorer for
its builder and date of building are unknown. The clues to its
origin lie in its plan and style; it is probably of the 13th century
and believed to have been a stronghold of the Comyns at the
time of the Wars of Independence. There is no doubt, however,
that it was a fortress of great strength at the time of its building.
There is also a tradition that it is the site of a great city in Pictish
times which was destroyed by the Danes. Inverlochy is also the

site of one of Montrose's battles against Argyle. After a tactical march of some 30 miles and over hills 2000 feet high, the Royalist force went on to defeat a government force twice their size. On this site is enough history and drama for any explorer.

LOCH AN EILEAN
H49

NH8907   *Aviemore*

A stronghold of the Wolf of Badenoch, the son of Robert II, this ruined castle stands on an island in Rothiemurcus forest. The whole setting is of great beauty contrasting sharply with the traditional tales of terror linked to the castles of the Wolf. The explorer will find this site well worth seeking out.

LOCH NAN UAMN
H50

NM7184   *Mallaig*

On 5th August 1745, Bonnie Prince Charlie landed on Scotland's mainland, stepping ashore on this remote spot in the Western Highlands. Today's explorer can arrive by car rather than a French ship. The place you seek on the shore is marked by a cairn.

LOCHINDORB CASTLE
H51

NH9736   *Grantown-on-Spey*

*'Whosoever holds Lochindorb Castle can control most
of the North-east.'*
JAMIE IN *A FOLLY OF PRINCES*

In the 13th century the castle was owned by the Comyns. It became the stronghold of The Wolf of Badenoch, from where he carried out his reign of terror. The castle occupies an entire island of one acre in Lochindorb, in the isolated Dava Moor. Originally built with round towers at each corner, only one tower and the walls now remain.

RANNOCH MOOR

NN3552

H54

Bridge of Orchy

A vast and dreary expanse of bog, peat hag and moor. The Tyndrum to Ballachulish road crosses by way of one side of the moor. However, the best way to see this huge desolate landscape is from the train from Crianlarich to Fort William.

TAIN

NH7982

H56

> *'They took refuge in the chapel. Of Saint Duthac. At Tain. A noted sanctuary — we caught him there...'*
>
> THE ROSSMAN TO ROBERT THE BRUCE IN THE PATH OF THE HERO KING

A former Royal Burgh and at one time the capital of Ross. The chapel of St Duthac, now a roofless ruin, was a sanctuary and it was from here that the Bruce's Queen Elizabeth was dragged and taken to England by the Earl of Ross. Amongst those who made the pilgrimage to the chapel was James IV.

URQUHART CASTLE

NH5228

H61

Drumnadrochit

> *'I have come for my castle,' Bruce went on. 'Yield it to me, Sir Alexander, as is your duty and right, and you may remain its keeper.'*
>
> ROBERT THE BRUCE IN THE PATH OF THE HERO KING

Standing on a promontory jutting into Loch Ness, with the waters lapping on three sides, this famous castle was virtually ruined before the rising of 1715, the buildings having been blown up to prevent their use by the Jacobites. Little is known of the origin of the castle; the ruins as seen today date from the early 16th century but there is evidence of the earlier fortress and royal garrison on the site. Heavily fortified, the castle sits in a strategic position in the Great Glen and during the reign of

Robert the Bruce the castle was stormed, plundered and changed hands four times.

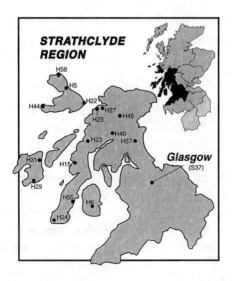

AROS

NM5645

H5

Tobermory

It was a celebration. Aros on the isle of Mull across the
sound from Ardtornish, was the first of Somerled's
new Norman-style castles.
LORD OF THE ISLES

Once a stronghold of the Lords of the Isles, little remains to reveal the great strength of what was a major fortification. It takes only a little imagination to re-inhabit the site with the warriors of Somerled, first Lord of the Isles and his successive generations.

ARRAN

NS0138

H6

Probably one of the best known of Scottish islands. Jumping off place for Robert the Bruce on his return from the Hebridean exile, it was from here he commenced the long campaign that led to victory. With the ancient castles of Brodick and Lochranza, bays used by the Vikings and the Lords of the Isles, its exploration is rewarding.

CASTLE SWEEN
NR7178

H15
Ardrishaig

'Welcome to my poor house, Lord Thane of Argyll' he
said carefully. 'I have heard much of you.'
SOMERLED IN LORD OF THE ISLES

High on a rock on the eastern shore of the sea loch, Loch Sween, stand the ruins of what has been described as the earliest stone castle in Scotland, probably built around the mid-12th century. Besieged and burned by Sir Alastair Macdonald, a lieutenant of Montrose in 1647, much still remains of the structure.

DUART CASTLE
NM7435

H22
Craignure

Built on a peninsula at the entrance to the Sound of Mull, this imposing stronghold of the Clan MacLean is thought to have been built about 1250 with later additions. After the Jacobite risings, the castle was commissioned as a garrison and became a ruin, being restored in the early part of this century.

DUNADD
NR8393

H23
Lochgilphead

...the isolated, conical hill of Dunadd, once the capital
of ancient Dalriada of the Scots.
CRUSADER

The ancient capital of the Scots of Dalriada. Now only a hillock and a rock carved with the image of a boar. This was once the fortress of the Scots who, coming from Ireland in the sixth century established their kingdom in Argyll. It was Kenneth MacAlpin, King of Scots who united the Picts and the Scots into one kingdom in AD839.

DUNAVERTY CASTLE
NR6807

H24

Campbeltown

> *To call the place an eagle's nest, a sea-eagle's nest was*
> *the feeblest inadequacy.*
> THE PATH OF THE HERO KING

Little now remains of this early stronghold, which stands on a pyramid of rock with a sheer drop to the sea. A castle of the Lords of the Isles, it was captured in 1493 by James IV and again by General Leslie in 1647 when he slaughtered the inhabitants.

DUNOLLIE CASTLE
NM8531

H25

Oban

The ruined ancient seat of the Macdougals of Lorn stands on a rocky outcrop overlooking Loch Etive between Oban and Dunstaffnage. The Keep or Donjon remain, along with fragments of older buildings.

DUNSTAFFNAGE CASTLE
NM8834

H27

Oban

> *'Go you back to Dunstaffnage in Lorn and await the*
> *outcome.'*
> KING ALEXANDER IN TRUE THOMAS

Standing on a high promontory in the Firth of Lorne, in a strategic position, the building work commenced in the 13th century by the MacDougal Lords of Lorne, and were added to in the 15th and 16th centuries. The castle was the first resting place in Scotland of the original Stone of Destiny before it was moved to Scone Palace.

DUNYVAIG CASTLE H29
NR4045 *Port Ellen*

The principal castle of the Macdonald descendants of Donald of Islay, grandson of Somerled, Lord of the Isles. Little is now left but its strong position shows how important it must once have been and it was the place from which 1000 Macdonald men left to fight at Bannockburn. The nearby village of Port Ellen is, in fact, a modern creation, the first house being built in 1824 by the Campbell laird.

FINLAGGAN CASTLE H31
NR3968 *Bowmore*

'He had heard the tale that the deposed but rightful
King of England had arrived, of all places, on the isle
of Islay, at Donald of the Isles' castle of Finlaggan.'
THE DUKE OF ROTHESAY IN *A FOLLY OF PRINCES*

On Eilean Mor in Loch Finlaggan in the north of Islay, the ruins of Finlaggan Castle and a chapel mark the remains of one of the principal strongholds of the Lords of the Isles. Finlaggan was a seat of government of the Lord of the Isles and on a second isle, Eilean na Comhairle, was the Council House of the Lordship, said to be the crowning place of the Lord of the Isles.

INVERARAY CASTLE H40
NN0908 *Inveraray*

Seat of the Dukes of Argyll and power base of the Clan Campbell, the present castle is more of a mansion house. From the middle of the 16th century, when the first castle was built, until 1770 the castle was a West Highland keep but after 1606 it was left to decay. However, the post-rebellion Dukes, always the 'King's men', were embroiled in the politics of London and needing a new power base in Scotland to match their importance, built the magnificent new castle and town thus sweeping away the old.

IONA H44
NM2724
This small island set off the south-west tip of Mull has been a place of pilgrimage for many centuries. Here St Columba settled about AD563 and established his base. The abbey of today is, of course, the restored building of the Benedictine Abbey of the middle ages. A visit to Iona is not only an exploration of what is probably the most important early Christian site in Scotland, but also of a major influence in the creation of Scotland as a nation.

KILCHURN CASTLE H45
NN1327 *Dalmally*
Standing on what is now a marsh that was once an island, Kilchurn is said to have been built by the wife of Sir Colin Campbell who was on a crusade at the time, and completed about 1440. A semi-ruin, it is sited in a position of awe-inspiring grandeur. It should, however, not be confused with the earlier castle of the Campbells still further down the loch at Portsonachan. Innischonnel Castle was the stronghold of the Bruce's friend, Sir Neil Campbell.

SADDAIL H55
NR7832 *Campbeltown*
'We go to Saddail, where my new Abbey is abuilding.'
SOMERLED IN LORD OF THE ISLES

The last remains of Somerled's abbey are to be found here. Founded in the 12th century, it was a Cistercian establishment. Close by stands the restored 16th century Saddell Castle.

TARBERT H57
NN3104
A name used in Scotland for an isthmus over which boats could be drawn. This Tarbert has a history of over 1200 years. Guarded by a castle that is recorded as being burned in AD712, the last in

the line was built about 1494 but is now a ruin. King Magnus Barefoot hauled his galleys across the isthmus, as did Robert the Bruce. In the 12th century this was part of the realm of Somerled, Lord of the Isles.

TOBERMORY   H58
NM5055

Founded by the British Society for Promoting the Fisheries of Scotland in 1788, the village of Tobermory overlooks one of the finest anchorages in the West of Scotland. This facility was much used by the Lords of the Isles, and it saw its share of fighting, pillage and plunder in the days of the Norsemen.

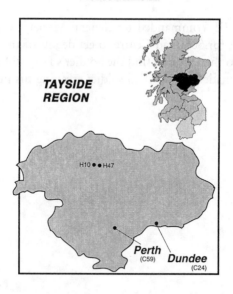

BLAIR ATHOLL H10
NN8765

An interesting highland village, but the main interest to the explorer must be Blair Castle. The oldest part of the castle dates to about 1270. It stands guard, in gleaming white, over the junction of the Rivers Garry and Tilt with their passes to the north. Seat of the Duke of Atholl, history is written into the very stones of the castle guarded by Scotland's only private army, the Atholl Highlanders.

KILLIECRANKIE H47
NN9063 *Pitlochry*

> *'A soldier takes failure and success as they come.'*
> GRAHAM OF CLAVERHOUSE IN *THE PATRIOT*

One of the most famous of Scottish battles took place in this area. The actual battlefield was on the high ground a little to the north of the Pass. It was here on the 27th July 1689 that the Jacobites of John Graham, Viscount Dundee, defeated the army of William III, commanded by General Mackay. Visit the National Trust for Scotland Centre to get details of the battle and go deep into the Pass and find the Soldier's Leap, site of a legendary jump made by a terrified soldier escaping his pursuers.

CENTRAL SCOTLAND

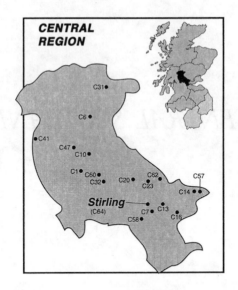

ABERFOYLE   C1
NN5201

Safe behind the great Flanders Moss, now drained, the clachan of Aberfoyle is deep in Rob Roy country. The village of today serves as your gateway to the Trossachs and Loch Lomondside with Rob Roy's cave a mile to the north of Inversnaid.

BALQUHIDDER   C6
NN5320   *Callander*

> *...From Balquhidder they crossed the passes above Glen*
> *Gyle and down Loch Katrine-side...*
> THE CAPTAIN GENERAL

Home of the MacLaren clan who suffered many raids by the MacGregors. Beside the roofless remains of the old church is the burial place of Rob Roy, his wife and two of his sons.

BANNOCKBURN
NS7990

C7
Stirling

> *'My Friends', he cried, arm raised when quiet was*
> *gained. 'Today we put all to the test. Today Scotland*
> *stands or falls.'*
> THE BRUCE BEFORE BANNOCKBURN IN THE PATH OF THE
> HERO KING

Village and site of the most famous battle in Scotland's history. Located astride the road from Falkirk to Stirling and commanding the route to Stirling Castle to the relief of which Edward II of England was marching. The Borestone in which the standard of Robert the Bruce was fixed is in the grounds of the National Trust for Scotland Heritage Centre. The probable site of the battle is due east of the Borestone and crossed by a road from St Ninians to the village of Bannockburn. This is not the traditional site which is closer to the Stirling to Grangemouth road. It is also in this area close to Bannockburn that James III was murdered in a building known as Beaton's Mill.

BRIG O'TURK
NN5306

C10
Callander

Bridge and hamlet on the road from Callander to the Trossachs and deep into the land of Rob Roy.

CAMBUSKENNETH ABBEY
NS8093

C13
Stirling

An abbey founded by David I on the left bank of the River Forth and sometimes referred to as the Monastery of Stirling. In 1326 the clergy and nobility met in the abbey to swear fealty to David Bruce as heir apparent in the presence of his father, King Robert the Bruce, who had here accepted the surrender of the English nobles after Bannockburn. Also the place of the marriage of King Robert's sister, Christian to Andrew Murray of Bothwell.

CASTLE CAMPBELL
NS9699

C14
Dollar

> *'He is not in Argyll. These last few weeks he has been
> at Castle Campbell, near Dollar. Not ten miles across
> the Ochils from your own house at Kincardine.'*
> SIR THOMAS HOPE IN *THE YOUNG MONTROSE*

Situated above the town of Dollar on a rocky outcrop on a spur of the Ochil Hills. Known originally as 'Castle Gloume', this fine castle was acquired by Colin Campbell, first Earl of Argyll, who changed the name by Act of Parliament in 1489 to Castle Campbell. There is a possibility that a Norman castle stood on the site during the 12th century.

CLACKMANNAN
NS9092

C16

For many generations known to be the seat of the Bruce family, the town stands in the plain of the River Forth. Robert the Bruce resided here before the Battle of Bannockburn and is thought to have built the tower which stands on King's Seat Hill, once the site of a royal hunting lodge. The tower is well preserved today. King David II spent the first part of his reign here and before his death donated it to a kinsman, Robert Bruce.

DOUNE CASTLE
NN7301

C20
Doune

> *'He invited this alleged Richard Plantagenet to his
> own castle of Doune, in Menteith.'*
> DUKE OF ROTHESAY IN *A FOLLY OF PRINCES*

The great stronghold of Robert and his son Murdoch, Dukes of Albany. Whilst the present castle is mainly of their building, the origins of the castle go back at least a century earlier for it was a seat of the Earls of Menteith. Restored in the 19th century, the old stones could tell many a tale spanning the five centuries from the 13th century to the Jacobite Rebellion.

DUNBLANE C23
NN7801

Standing on the banks of the River Allan is the ancient cathedral thought to have been founded by David I in 1142. Following damage during the Reformation the building was left without a roof and stood for 300 years as a ruin until it was restored in the late 19th century. Five denominations have used the cathedral for worship and when used by the Episcopal church in the 17th century, Bishop Leighton was elevated to become Archbishop of Glasgow. He bequeathed his personal library to the diocese for the use of the clergy and this expanded collection can be seen today in the Leighton Library near to the Cathedral.

FINLARIG CASTLE C31
NN5733 *Killin*

Near to the village of Killin are the ruins of the ancient seat of the Campbells of Breadalbane.

FLANDERS MOSS C32
NS5096 *Stirling*

> *'But if a north-west wind off yon hielant hills sweeps down over Flanders Moss and hits this castle-rock, there could be down-draughts that could flatten this frail canopy.'*
> *JAMIE IN A FOLLY OF PRINCES*

To the north of the Campsie and Fintry Hills and to the west of Stirling lies the giant Flanders Moss. Now drained, the moss provided an impenetrable barrier to all except the few who knew the secret of the safe tracks across it. Said to have covered 10,000 acres or more, the moss certainly served as a protective moat to the Trossachs and the Macgregors of Rob Roy.

INVERSNAID
NN3308

C41

Aberfoyle

On the east shore of Loch Lomond with fine views of the surrounding countryside. About one mile north is the cave where Rob Roy took refuge from his assailants. In the early 18th century a barracks was built to repress the Highlanders and in particular the MacGregors, who attacked and burned it several times. Until the late 1800s the only access was across a bleak, dangerous moor from Aberfoyle but there is now a good road. A hotel has been established here for some time.

LOCH KATRINE
NN4907

C47

Aberfoyle

The centre of the famed Trossachs and deep in Rob Roy country. A passenger boat, the SS Sir Walter Scott, plies the loch, giving a changing view of the wilds.

OCHIL HILLS
NN9904

C57

Dollar

Stretching eastwards from Stirling, these hills form a great barrier between Fife and Strathearn. They tower above the countryside producing a near highland landscape. Glen Devon with its castle is the main pass through them.

OLD SAUCHIE
NS7888

C58

Stirling

It was in this area that a battle, overshadowed in history by the nearby Bannockburn, was fought. 11th June 1488 saw the defeat of James III and his assassination in the long forgotten battle of Beaton's Mill. The site of the mill can be found by following the trail from Bannockburn village.

PORT OF MENTEITH C60
NN5801

At the northern corner of the Lake of Menteith, this village port serves as the take-off point to visit the island priory of Inchmahome — a ferry boat, islands housing a priory, castle and dog kennels, all providing a rich tapestry of history — what more could an explorer want?

SHERIFFMUIR C62
NN8202 *Dunblane*

The 13th November 1715 saw the Battle of Sheriffmuir between the troops of King George I and the supporters of the Old Pretender. Neither side was victorious for the right wing of each army broke the left wing of its opponent's forces and at the end of the day everyone retired quietly from the field. Situated high on the north side of the Ochils to the east of Dunblane, it is still a wild and open moor. The three boulders marking the spot where the Jacobite standard was raised should be sought out.

STIRLING C64
NS7894

The fortress town at the waist of Scotland dominated by its castle, has played a major role in the nation's story.

Stirling Castle, one Scotland's most important fortresses

Guarding the only crossing point of the River Forth for an army in medieval times, the town has witnessed some of the major events in Scottish history. Explore the great castle, seek out Wallace's sword at the Wallace Monument, find the Beheading Stone, the Church of the Holy Rude and the Bastion beneath the modern shopping centre. The battlefields of Stirling Bridge and Bannockburn are nearby.

BALMERINO

C5

NO3524   *Wormit*

A former fishing village on the south bank of the River Tay. The lands of Balmerino were purchased in 1225 by the mother of Alexander II, Queen Emengarde, who founded a Cistercian abbey and on her death in 1233 she was buried there. The abbey was raided by the English in 1547 and although repaired, it again suffered damage during the Reformation. The ruins of this once majestic building can still be seen.

CULROSS

C19

NS9885

> *'The Keldei at Culross are the best beekeepers in the land. They keep the Queen's bees for her. And make the palace candles with their wax.'*
> MALDRED IN MARGARET THE QUEEN

High over the town are the ruins of Culross Abbey, founded in 1217 by Malcolm, Thane of Fife, and the chapel of which is now the Parish Church. On the shore road are fragments of a chapel built on the spot where St Mungo, founder of Glasgow Cathedral was born to Thanea, daughter of King Loth of the Picts.

DUNFERMLINE   C25
NT1087

> *'That is where the King has his tower and palace. At*
> *the dun. Dun Farlane — it has become changed to*
> *Dunfermline.'*
> *MALDRED IN MARGARET THE QUEEN*

Now a busy industrial town in the Kingdom of Fife, Dunfermline was once the home of many of the Scottish kings. The town developed round the Benedictine abbey built by David I in 1128, on the site of Queen Margaret's original church, founded between 1070 and 1086 which can be located in the present nave. Her shrine can be seen near the east gate where it has been since 1250. Within the area of the abbey, but outside the building are the resting places of her husband Malcolm Canmore and their sons: King Edgar, Alexander I and his queen; David I and his two wives; Malcolm IV and Alexander III, his queen and son. During reconstruction work in 1818, the tomb of Robert the Bruce was discovered. The skeletal body was dressed in robes considered to be royal and the breast-bone had marks showing where the heart had been removed. On his death-bed, King Robert asked that his heart be taken on a Crusade, but the bearer, Sir James Douglas, was killed in battle at Zebas de Ardales in Spain on 25th March 1330. The King's heart was recovered and taken to Melrose Abbey for burial.

Falkland Palace, where Mary Queen of Scots found refuge during her turbulent reign

FALKLAND C29
NO2507 *Auchtermuchty*

Nothing now remains of Falkland Castle, the early residence of the Earls of Fife but the site was used for Falkland Palace, a royal hunting lodge thought to have been built by James III and enlarged and embellished by both James IV and James V, the latter of whom held court and died here of a broken heart. His widow, Mary of Guise, often resided here with her infant daughter, Mary Queen of Scots who also sought refuge in the palace during her reign. James VI was in residence in 1600 when the Gowrie conspiracy took place.

FIFE C30
NO2006

The Kingdom of Fife from Forth to Tay is almost a world to itself. Exploration of its coast will take you from the days of the Druids at Culross to the Castle of St. Andrews. Inland you can travel from the Palace of Falkland to the ruins of Lindores Abbey and the Pictish tower of Abernethy. Individual places are named in the guide.

Inchcolm – an important Druidic site that can be visited today by a boat from South Queensferry

INCHCOLM ISLAND
NT1882

C39
Aberdour

A holy place since the days of the Druids, its original name was Pemona, meaning the Island of Druids. The remains of a Culdee cell and the Augustinian monastery tell more of its story.

LINDORES ABBEY
NO2616

C46
Newburgh

Near Newburgh on the southern banks of the River Tay are to be found the remains of a Benedictine Abbey founded by David, Earl of Huntingdon towards the end of the 12th century and of great historical importance. Approximately two miles from the ruins of the Abbey at the end of Lindores Loch is the site of a castle which is reputed to have belonged to Macduff, the first Thane of Fife. In this vicinity in 1300, William Wallace fought a victorious battle against the English army and retired to the castle.

LOMOND HILLS C50
NO2006 *Auchtermuchty*

> *The view from the Lomond ridge was extensive,*
> *magnificent. Southwards, across the gleaming firth, all*
> *Lothian lay spread, green and fertile.*
> MACBETH THE KING

Rising to the south of Falkland Palace, these hills dominate central Fife. They were once a part of the great Royal Forest, and a favourite hunting ground of James VI. The trees of this forest were cut down in 1652 on the orders of Cromwell for use in the construction of a fort at Dundee. A road cuts through the hills from Falkland to Leslie.

MAY, ISLE OF C52
NT6599 *Anstruther*

> *Gazing, the Isle of May became a symbol of hope.*
> THANEA IN DRUID SACRIFICE

The remains of a 13th century chapel are dedicated to St Adrian who was killed on the isle by Danish raiders in the 9th century. This can be reached by boat from Anstruther.

The ruins of the ancient castle of St Andrews where Robert the Bruce convened his first Parliament

ST ANDREWS C63
NO5016

Known today as the golfing capital of the world, St Andrews has played a major role in Scotland's story. See the castle overlooking the North Sea which was the scene of the first Parliament convened by Robert the Bruce, the nearby ruins of the cathedral and Augustinian priory and the church of St Rule with its high square tower. St Mary's College, Scotland's oldest university college, was founded in 1411 by Bishop Wardlaw.

WEMYSS C67
NT3295

The caves of Wemyss have a history dating back to the days of the Druids and before. Regretfully the Pictish wall paintings, for which the caves are famous, are now in great danger from erosion.

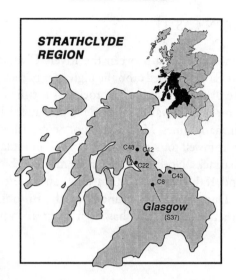

BARDOWIE CASTLE⚘   C8
NS5773   *Milngavie*

An early 16th century castle with later additions standing beside Bardowie Loch, close to Milngavie. A seat of the Galbraith family, it passed to ancestors of the Dukes of Hamilton. In 1707 John Hamilton's sister Mary married Gregor 'Black Knee' Macgregor, Rob Roy's nephew.

BUCHANAN CASTLE   C12
NS4688   *Drymen*

Overlooking Endrick Water as it flows into Loch Lomond, the castle has associations with Rob Roy. Nothing now remains of the structure, and its grounds are part of Buchanan Castle golf course.

DUMBARTON CASTLE   C22
NS4074   *Dumbarton*

Standing on a peninsula between the Rivers Clyde and Leven, Dumbarton Castle perched atop the high, craggy rock is a prominent feature of the landscape. The rock was fortified by the Romans, became a medieval royal castle and changed hands with the English many times. Mary Queen of Scots visited the castle as a child. Cromwell took possession in 1652 and it later became a military barracks. Nothing is left of the medieval buildings but the 17th and 18th century fortifications can be seen. Since the time when Dumbarton was founded by the Britons, the town has been a strategic site and has been of great importance to seafarers.

KILSYTH   C43
NS7478

The Battle of Kilsyth was on 15th August 1645 and ended in a great victory for Montrose and the Royalists. The battlefield is found directly to the east of the town. A minor road crosses it from the A803 to Banton. Part of the area is now a reservoir. Visit Colzium House to find relics of the battle.

LOCH LOMOND   C48
NS3597   *Balloch*

> *David, for one, almost felt a holiday atmosphere*
> *prevailing as he proceeded up the lovely banks of Loch*
> *Lomond.*
>
> DAVID DE LINDSAY IN CRUSADER

The greatest stretch of inland water in the UK. At its southern end, the island of Inchmurrin has on it the ruins of the castle of the Earls of Lennox and the one time seat of the earldom. At the other end of the loch we find the land of the MacGregors, Inversnaid and Rob Roy's cave.

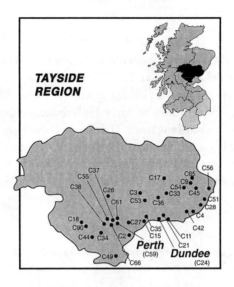

ABERNETHY C2
NO1916

> *There is still a strange round tower there, only one*
> *other like it in the land. Tall and slender.*
>
> CRUSADER

The present town gives little indication of its ancient past. Probably a royal residence founded about AD600 and said to have been 'the chief seat, both regal and fortifical, of the whole kingdom of the Picts'. It was also a principal seat of the Culdees. At Abernethy Malcolm Canmore was forced to do homage to William the Conqueror in 1072. To the south-west you will find the Castle Law while to the north-east is 'Carpow' the Roman fortress and port. In the centre of the town you will discover the 74ft high Round Tower, one of only two in Scotland.

ALYTH   C3
NO2448

A quiet and sleepy country town at the entrance to Glen Isla and on the edge of the Grampian foothills. But the area has its place in history for tradition says that Queen Guinevra, wife of King Arthur, was held prisoner at Barry Hill, the castle or fort some 1½ miles north-east of the town. To the west is the Ramsay stronghold of Bamff Castle, while to the north, deep into Glen Isla is the recently restored Forter Castle, a tower which belonged to the Ogilvies and was burned by the Duke of Argyle in 1640.

ARBROATH   C4
NO6341

'I am a baillie and justiciar of the Abbey of Arbroath.
As my father was before me.'
ALEXANDER LINDSAY IN BLACK DOUGLAS

A busy fishing port on the North Sea, Arbroath is of particular importance in Scottish history. View the imposing ruins of the Abbey, founded in 1178 by William the Lion and the seat of the Scottish Parliament during the reign of King Robert the Bruce where the Declaration of Independence addressed to Pope John XXII was prepared and signed.

BRECHIN CASTLE   C9
NO5960   *Brechin*

Built on the site of an ancient castle on a perpendicular rock overhanging the River South Esk, Brechin Castle is the seat of the Earl of Dalhousie. In 1303 it was the site of a siege by the English under Edward I for 20 days. Despite every effort to hold out, the Governor, Sir Thomas Maule was killed by a stone and the place immediately fell to the enemy.

The round tower and Cathedral of Brechin

BROUGHTY CASTLE   C11
NO4630   *Dundee*
See under Dundee

CASTLE HUNTLY   C15
NO3029   *Dundee*

> *The Lord Gray came home to Castle Huntly in a gale*
> *of wind and the worst of tempers.*
> THE COURTESAN

See under Dundee

CORTACHY CASTLE✜

NO3959

C17

Kirriemuir

> 'How many days, Jamie? And nights?'
> 'Nine. Ten at the most. All must be at Cortachy by St
> Gregory's Eve, 11th of March, at latest.'
> MARY STEWART TO JAMIE IN *A FOLLY OF PRINCES*

A 15th century Z-plan castle of the Ogilvys. The previous 14th century castle of the Earls of Strathearn has entirely disappeared and the present castle has been rebuilt twice having been destroyed by fire on both occasions.

CRIEFF

NN8621

C18

Now mainly a residential town, Crieff was from 1672 until 1770 the site of the great annual market or cattle tryst for the whole of Scotland. The fame of the 'kind gallows of Crieff' where the sentences of the Seneschals of the King's Estate of Strathearn were carried out was spread far and wide. Nothing remains of the old town of Crieff for it was razed to the ground by the Jacobites.

DUDHOPE CASTLE

NO3930

C21

Dundee

See under Dundee

DUNDEE

NO4030

C24

> 'If I knew that I was dealing with James Graham of
> Montrose, I'd turn and ride for Dundee as though
> Auld Nick was at my tail!'
> PATE GRAHAM IN *THE CAPTAIN GENERAL*

The present city of Dundee is mainly a mixture of Victorian and modern buildings, but hidden away may still be found a number of places of historic significance. For the explorer the first place to aim for must be the Law — the hill that dominates the city. From its summit the whole panorama of the Tay estuary, the city and surrounding countryside is spread out before you. Seek out the City Churches with the Tower of St Marys or Old Steeple, Dudhope Castle (the castle of the Scrimgeours, hereditary standard bearers to the King of Scots), Mains Castle, and Claypotts Castle. Situated at the old crossing point of the Tay estuary, Broughty Castle is in a position of considerable strength, and occupies the point called Broughty Craig. The construction of the castle was probably commenced in 1490 as the then Lord Gray of Fowlis received a licence to build a fortified tower on the rock. The castle saw much warfare during the following hundred years and seems to have eventually fallen into disuse and ruin. It was rebuilt and equipped by the War Office in 1855. It should be noted that Castle Huntly is also near at hand just to the west of the city and clearly visible from the Dundee to Perth road. Built in 1452 by Andrew, Lord Grey of Fowlis, the massive tower of Castle Huntly dominates the surrounding area of the Carse of Gowrie.

DUNKELD   C26
NO0242
A little town with a long history of more than 1000 years. Originally a Culdee establishment succeeded by a monastery, it was joined by a church built by Kenneth MacAlpin. In 1318 the original building was commenced with the choir and during the next 200 years, the complete cathedral developed only to be destroyed in 1560 during the Reformation. Behind the altar is the tomb of the notorious Wolf of Badenoch, Alexander Stewart, Earl of Buchan, third son of Robert II. In 1390 the Wolf burned Forres and sacked and burned Elgin Cathedral as part of a reign of terror in the north. In the early 1400s a castle was built but all trace of it has now gone. The origins of this most attractive town go back to Celtic times, the Picts regarded it as an important

place and Kenneth made it a joint capital with Scone. The town suffered in the aftermath of the Battle of Killiecrankie. Latterly, it gained much popularity through its associations with Queen Victoria on her highland visits.

DUNSINANE   C27
NO2131   *Perth*

> *...and its name, dun-sithean, the mound or fort of the*
> *fairies.*
> MACBETH THE KING

The hill and one time fortress which tradition claims was the stronghold of Macbeth. The flat summit of the hill shows the remains of what must have been a formidable rampart that may well have surrounded a hall-house of considerable size. In addition to the Macbeth connection, local tradition has it that the true Stone of Destiny was hidden on the hill when Edward I plundered Scone Abbey and removed a rough block of local sandstone instead.

ETHIE CASTLE⚓   C28
NO6846   *Arbroath*
In 1530 Ethie was inhabited by the Abbot of Arbroath, later Cardinal Beaton who was to be murdered at knife-point in the Sea-Tower of St Andrews Castle in 1546. With his death a period of dramatic and bloody action in Scotland's history was most aptly portrayed. The modest castle later grew, as the seat of the Earls of Northesk, into a large and rambling mansion house.

FORFAR CASTLE   C33
NO4550   *Forfar*
Little is known of the form and type of this castle, now marked by a modern tower, but it is considered to have been of great importance and a royal residence in the early 11th century. Malcolm Canmore held a parliament here in 1057 when surnames

were first conferred on the nobility. His queen, Margaret, had a residence built for religious retreat on an island in Forfar Loch. In the late 18th century it is said that the weapons used by the murderers of Malcolm II at Glamis were found in the loch.

FORTEVIOT   C34
NO0517   *Dundee*

> *'The King has houses, palaces, at Forteviot and*
> *Dunsinane and Kincardine.'*
> MALDRED IN MARGARET THE QUEEN

Once the capital of the Pictish kingdom of Fortrenn, the present village is slightly to the south-east of the original site. Between the death of Kenneth in AD860 and the 14th century, the palace and later castle seems to have been in continuous occupation. All trace of this important centre has now disappeared.

FOULIS CASTLE   C35
NO3332   *Dundee*

> *'Where is thy noble and puissant Lord Gray?'* Patrick
> *asked lightly.*
> *'He is at Foulis castle. Has been for some days.'*
> DAVID IN LORD AND MASTER

The castle of Foulis was at one time the seat of the Lords Gray. Situated at Easter Fowlis, it is one of three of that name, the others being Fowlis Wester, near Crieff and Foulis Castle in Ross-shire. In its heyday it was a powerful stronghold of the courtyard type. Now all that remains is a three-storey tower house.

GLAMIS CASTLE   C36
NO3848   *Forfar*

One of the ancient royal palaces of Scotland and the place of murder of Malcolm II, or so legend says. A royal hunting lodge that stood on the site was given to Sir John Lyon in 1370 when he was made Thane of Glamis and the lands and estates of Glamis have remained in the family of Bowes Lyon ever since. The building of Glamis Castle as it is today seems to have commenced in the early 15th century and is the result of nearly 600 years development. Glamis is, of course, the family home of Queen Elizabeth, the Queen Mother.

HUNTINGTOWER CASTLE C37
NO0825 *Perth*

'Inverness sacked. My castles of Urquhart and
Ruthven stormed, my servants slain.'
JAMES STEWART IN BLACK DOUGLAS

On the banks of the River Almond three miles west of Perth, this old building, formerly known as Ruthven Castle was the seat of the Gowrie family who conspired with other protestant nobles in 1582 and imprisoned the young King James VI in the castle while they misruled the country. The building of today probably dates from the 15th century but has been added to throughout the years.

INCHAFFREY ABBEY C38
NN9522 *Methven*

'He is gone today to Inchaffrey. To speak with the
Lord Madderty. Awaiting your return. He will be
back anon. We ride tomorrow.'
MAGDALEN IN THE YOUNG MONTROSE

Little now remains of the ancient Celtic priory founded in 1200 by Gilbert, Earl of Strathearn and his Countess, Matilda, on the banks of the Pow Water. It was richly endowed by Gilbert and his successors and gained many privileges from King David and King Alexander. Mauritius, Abbot of Inchaffrey, served Robert the Bruce at the Battle of Bannockburn and carried with him the arm of St Fillan, one of the precious possessions of the abbey.

INNERPEFFRAY   C40
NN9018   *Crieff*

A small and apparently obscure library, but of interest to the explorer because of its connection with the Marquis of Montrose. Founded by one of Montrose's officers, David Drummond, Lord Madderty, it contains a wonderful collection of books including Montrose's personal pocket Bible. Nearby is the castle of Lord Madderty.

KELLY CASTLE   C42
NO6040   *Arbroath*

Built upon a rock on a bank of the River Elliot near to Arbroath, the present castle is on the site of an early mansion. Initially home to the Mowbrays and then passed to a Stewart supporter of Bruce until 1402 when it came to the Ochterlonys, it was known as such for two centuries until acquired by the Irvine family in the early 1600s.

KINCARDINE CASTLE   C44
NN9411   *Auchterarder*

> *'King Alexander sent me from Kincardine Castle. To*
> *look to and steward his baronies of Monymusk, Fyvie,*
> *Drum and Darnaway.'*
> THOMAS IN TRUE THOMAS

Situated in Kincardine Glen near to Auchterarder, this ancient seat of the Graham family was burned to the ground in 1646 and never rebuilt.

KINNAIRD CASTLE ⚓   C45
NO6356   *Montrose*

Home of the Earl of Southesk and closely associated with the Marquis of Montrose who was married to the daughter of the first Earl. The castle underwent extensive alterations in the 1860s and is not open to the public.

Loch Leven Castle with the Lomond Hills in the background

LOCH LEVEN CASTLE   C49
NO1301   *Kinross*

> *'This is the true deed of abdication, then? Signed by her*
> *own hand at Lochleven. In July, 1567. Twenty years*
> *ago. And all these years this has existed – the proof*
> *that I needed! That she has indeed abdicated – signed*
> *with her own hand!'*
>
> ELIZABETH I IN LORD AND MASTER

Standing on an island at the north end of Loch Leven, which is overlooked from the busy Edinburgh to Perth road at Kinross, is this gloomy castle. Once the prison of Mary Queen of Scots, the castle can be reached during the summer months by a ferry from Kinross.

LUNAN BAY   C51
NO7051   *Montrose*

This attractive bay has as its focal point the castle ruin beside the Lunan Water. Redcastle was, according to local tradition, built by William the Lion as a hunting seat.

MEIGLE   C53
NO2844

A tiny village with an outstanding collection of Pictish stones from the early days of Scottish Christianity. The churchyard is claimed to have connections with Queen Guinevra (c. AD500) while Belmont Park nearby is reputed to have been the site of a battle between MacBeth and MacDuff.

MELGUND CASTLE   C54
NO5456   *Arbroath*

Connected to one of the most outstanding characters in Scottish history, Cardinal David Beaton built it about 1540 for his mistress Margaret Ogilvy. The ruins indicate a house of comfort and convenience as well as a strong tower. Search out the marriage stone with DB and MO marked on it.

METHVEN CASTLE ⚓   C55
NO0426   *Methven*

'Would that I could exchange it all for the good clean
air of Methven and the Hills of Strathearn!'
VICKY IN THE COURTESAN

A beautifully restored castle standing high above Strathearn the present structure dates from the early 17th century, but would seem to contain the remains of an earlier building. Before 1323 the lands of Methven belonged to the Mowbray family, who backed the wrong side in the War of Independence. For a long time the lands remained in the hands of the Crown before being given to the first Duke of Lennox in 1584. On his death they passed to his son, the second Duke who built the castle of today.

MONTROSE CASTLE   C56
NO7157   *Montrose*

An ancient castle on the summit of Fort-hill is said to have been the scene of King John Balliol's humiliation when he was forced to divest his robes and crown to Edward of England in 1296. In 1330 Sir James Douglas sailed from the port of Montrose on a Crusade with the heart of Robert the Bruce.

The ancient town of Perth – central to many episodes in Scottish history

PERTH   C59
NO1024

> '*Aye, Perth lies undefended. We could take it this night. All Baillie's stores, ammunition, cannon will be there.*'
>
> MONTROSE IN *THE CAPTAIN GENERAL.*

In the Middle Ages St John's Town was a place of importance.

Now St John's Kirk is virtually the sole surviving relic of the town of Wallace, Robert the Bruce and the early Stewart kings. In 1396 the ferocious Battle of the Clans took place on the North Inch. Clans Chattan and Kay fought to the bitter end before King Robert III and his court. The street names, wall plaques and markers will, however, help with the exploration of the town's historic and at times violent past.

SCONE   C61
NO1126   *Perth*

> *And this was the resting place of the Lia Faill, the*
> *famous Stone of Destiny, talisman of the race, the*
> *Abbot of Scone its keeper.*
> MACBETH THE KING

Once the capital of the Pictish kingdom and the residence of the Scottish kings, Scone Palace stands on the banks of the River Tay, some two miles from Perth. The Stone of Destiny, brought to Scone from Dunstaffnage in AD834 by Kenneth MacAlpin was used at coronations of the kings of Scotland until it was plundered. Edward I took to England what he thought to be the true Stone. An Augustinian abbey, which contained the stone, was built on the site of the Culdee chapel by Alexander I and later set alight by a mob after John Knox preached a sermon against popery in St John's Kirk in Perth. See also Boot Hill, a grassy mound reputed to have been formed when the noblemen brought some earth from their land to enable them to witness the crowning of the king whilst standing on their own land.

STRACATHRO   C65
NO6265   *Brechin*
A quiet and peaceful area that was the scene of battle in 1130. There are no traces to mark the site, nor are there any remains of the church in which Edward I forced John Balliol to do homage and thus divest Scotland of her independence in 1296.

TIBBERMORE   C66
NO0623   *Perth*

The name given to a battle on 1st September 1644. The Marquis
of Montrose routed the Covenanters who far outnumbered him.
The battle stretched across the open countryside from the A9
road near Dupplin to the village of Methven.

SOUTHERN SCOTLAND

ANCRUM S4
NT6224 *Jedburgh*

About two miles to the north of the village the battle of Ancrum Moor was fought in 1545, when a strong invading English force was defeated in 1567.

COLDINGHAM MOOR S16
NT8667 *Coldingham*

His scouts had been watching Coldingham Moor all
day.
BLACK DOUGLAS

The eastern route into Scotland. An area of approximately nine miles in length between Eyemouth and Cockburnspath in Berwickshire, containing ridges of the Lammermuir Hills. Being a bleak and joyless place, it was at one time a great hazard for travellers. In the village of Coldingham are the remains of the priory which was founded in 1098 by King Edgar of Scotland.

COLDSTREAM   S17
NT8439

The modern town of Coldstream stands where the old ford crossed the River Tweed at the mouth of the Leet Water. The castle, or rather its mound, that guarded the ford can be found on the south bank at Wark. This castle was an English stronghold and changed hands many times.

CRANSHAWS TOWER   S19
NT6861   *Duns*

A former stronghold of the Douglas family, this interesting 'castle' stands about one mile from Cranshaws Church.

DRYBURGH ABBEY   S23
NT5931   *St Boswells*

One of the famous Border monasteries, and standing on a horseshoe bend of the River Tweed, Dryburgh was founded about 1152 by Hugh de Morville. Due to the closeness of the border, little remains of the church but the cloister buildings have survived remarkably well.

The ruins of Dryburgh Abbey. Remnants of the cloister buildings still survive to this day

EARLSTON
S26
NT5738

The Ercildoune of history passed into the possession of the Earls of Dunbar and the ancient name was corrupted into the present 'Earlston'. Nothing remains of the Earls' castle, but the ruins of the Rhymer's Tower of True Thomas can still be found to the south of the village.

EILDON HILLS
S28
NT5432
Melrose

The three tops of the Eildons stand out in isolation above Melrose Abbey in the heart of the Borders and are famous as the meeting place of True Thomas of Ercildoune and the Queen of the Fairies. They are also said to contain a cave wherein King Arthur and the Knights of the Round Table sleep awaiting the call to arms.

Melrose Abbey nestling beneath the Eildon Hills

ETTRICK FOREST   S30
NT3524   *Selkirk*

'Where is...home? Ettrick, of course. Newark, in the
Forest. Where else?'
WILL IN BLACK DOUGLAS

A historical name for the chief part of Selkirkshire, Ettrick Forest is the remains of the great Caledonian Forest which covered most of the county and parts of Peeblesshire. During the English invasions the timber was severely depleted. The forest was granted to the Douglases by King Robert the Bruce but was forfeited in the 15th century, when it became a hunting ground. In the early 1500s James V converted the forest to sheep-pastures, which still remain today.

EYEMOUTH   S31
NT9464
An ancient seaport at the mouth of the River Eye, with a busy working harbour and fish market. Overlooking the sweeping sandy bay on the northern headland is the fort, the site of a fortification erected by the Duke of Somerset in his invasion of Scotland. The southern end of the bay is protected by a ridge of rocks known as the Harkers (or Hurcars). In the great gale of 1881, half of the fishing fleet from Eyemouth were lost and 129 men drowned.

FAST CASTLE   S33
NT8671   *Cockburnspath*
Rising from a pinnacle of rock jutting from the North Sea on the Berwickshire coast, Fast Castle was a grim and fearsome place connected to the land only by a drawbridge. Now only a fragment of a ruin but once a tower surrounded by flanking walls, it is approached by a narrow track dropping down the cliff face from Coldingham Moor. The final approach is now across a concrete causeway only a few feet wide with a drop of some 70ft

on either side. Known to have had at times a stormy history the castle was, in the time of James VI, the stronghold of Logan of Restalrig, one of the most notorious characters of the age. There are stories of hidden gold going back to Logan's time and the rock itself contains a large cavern but no way of entering it from the castle has, as yet, been discovered.

FERNIHIRST CASTLE   S34
NT6517   *Jedburgh*

On the banks of the Jed Water, the first Fernihirst Castle was built in the late 1400s but as a Border stronghold it was destroyed on a number of occasions by both the English and the Scots themselves. The home of the Kerr family throughout a long and turbulent period of Border history, the present castle dates in part back to 1598. A great deal of restoration has been done over the past 60 years, and the Kerr chief, the Marquis of Lothian, still resides here.

Hermitage Castle, one of the Border country's most forbidding fortresses

HERMITAGE CASTLE S41
NY6996 *Newcastleton*

Comyn, Earl of Menteith built the first castle which is known to have existed before 1296. The present building was probably started about 1338 and reconstructed before 1388; some remnants of the building remain as part of the present castle. The massive building stands in wild Border country, a grim and forbidding fortress with a history to match.

JEDBURGH S43
NT6520

A border town that, like the others, has suffered devastation through the years. The original castle was demolished in 1409 but the great abbey still stands as does Mary Queen of Scots' house. Little else of antiquity is evident. However, to explore the town and surrounding area is to dig deep in the history of the Borders. The town has had many visitors, among them the Romans. Masons constructed a church here in the 9th century, Scots and English fought interminably in bloody affrays, Alexander III married here and his death a year later led to the Wars of Independence. Mary Queen of Scots rode to Hermitage Castle from Jedburgh and Prince Charlie stayed here while marching south.

KELSO S44
NT7233

> *'There has been no burning, no sacking, no ravishing.*
> *I have used all in my path kindly. As the Abbots of*
> *Kelso, Dryburgh and Melrose. I have no wish to fight*
> *the Scots.'*
> HENRY IV IN A FOLLY OF PRINCES

Now a busy market town, Kelso is reputed to have been described by Sir Walter Scott as one of the most beautiful and romantic villages of Scotland.

The old bridge at Kelso. The town was one of Sir Walter Scott's favourites

The majestic ruins of one of the four famous Border abbeys stand in the town. Established by David I in the early 12th century, the Abbey has been despoiled and destroyed during the raids on the Borders by the English armies. In 1152, Henry, the only son of David I, died at Roxburgh Castle and was interred with much pomp in the Abbey. Seized in 1296 by Edward I, full restitution was made by a treaty between Robert Bruce and Edward III in 1328. When a cannon exploded at Roxburgh Castle in 1460, killing James II, his infant son was carried to the Abbey to be crowned James III. In 1545 an army led by the Earl of Hertford marched on Teviotdale; Kelso and its abbey were plundered and suffered much damage.

LAUDER   S48
NT5247
A small town said to have been a royal burgh since the reign of William the Lion. The site of the original castle of Thirlestane is two miles to the east of the present building. Thirlestane Castle, the great mansion house stands close by the town. On one of the main invasion routes into Scotland, the origins of the present magnificent building lie in a fort built by Edward I and said to be incorporated into the present building.

NEWARK CASTLE S53
NT4229 *Selkirk*

A massive Border stronghold standing on a steep bank of the Yarrow Water four miles above Selkirk and originally a royal hunting seat within the Forest of Ettrick. The Scotts of Buccleuch were the hereditary keepers. The castle was besieged and taken by the English under Lord Grey in 1548 and was the scene of a massacre of prisoners from Montrose's army, captured at the Battle of Philiphaugh. Troops from Cromwell's army occupied the castle after the Battle of Dunbar.

PHILIPHAUGH S56
NT4427 *Selkirk*

Here beside the Yarrow you will find the haugh or plain on which the Marquis of Montrose met total defeat at the hands of the Covenant army commanded by General Leslie. Best explored in conjunction with Selkirk, a plaque marks the house in West Port where the Marquis spent the night before the battle.

ROXBURGH CASTLE S61
NT7031 *Kelso*

The bridge served Roxburgh Castle across Teviot, my Lord. All who travel to Roxburgh, from the south, from Berwick, even from Kelso, must use it.'
ROBERT STEWART IN *A FOLLY OF PRINCES*

Once a great Border fortress, where the River Teviot joins the River Tweed, now all that remains are a few grassy mounds and bits of stone. The scene of many stirring events during its long history, it may well have been originally built by the Saxons to control that area of the Northumbrian kingdom. David I seems to have been the first monarch to have spent a great deal of time at Roxburgh. From then on it changed hands on many occasions. In 1460 it was the cause of the death of James II, who while conducting a siege of the castle was overseeing the firing of a cannon called the Lion when it exploded. The Queen, Mary of Guelder, took over control of the seige and so inspired the Scottish army that the garrison was forced to surrender. So that it might never again fall into English hands, the Scots themselves then reduced it to a pile of rubble.

SELKIRK CASTLE S63
NT4728 *Selkirk*

A royal castle used as a hunting lodge by the Saxon kings, Selkirk Castle was not of sufficiently durable construction to withstand the elements and nothing of it remains today. David I stayed at the castle but preferred the more secure Roxburgh castle. William the Lion and his son and grandson, Alexander II and Alexander III were occasional visitors but it ceased to be a royal residence before the accession of Robert the Bruce. In 1113 a colony of Tyronesian monks settled near the castle and remained there for some years before moving to Kelso Abbey.

SMAILHOLM TOWER S64
NT6334 *Kelso*

A Border tower set upon low crags which can be seen from many a mile distant. Built in the early 16th century, it takes but little imagination to see the watchman stand and stare towards the south.

ST ABBS HEAD S66
NT9169 *Coldingham*

The soaring rocks, nearly 300ft high, mark the site of St Ebbas Nunnery, founded by the daughter of the king of Northumberland in gratitude for her salvation from shipwreck upon the coast here. The whole headland is now a spectacular nature reserve.

SWINTON CASTLE ✦   S67
NT8147   *Coldstream*
It would seem that Swinton House is on the site of the original
castle. The Swintons of Swinton go back to the times before
records commenced and the family still occupy the present house.

THIRLESTANE CASTLE   S69
NT8028   *Lauder*
See under Lauder

YARROW VALLEY   S77
NT3527   *Selkirk*
With Philiphaugh at its eastern entrance, the valley leads to the
wild centre of an immense area and includes the ruined Newark
Castle of the Douglases and Dryhope Tower, close by St Mary's
Loch.

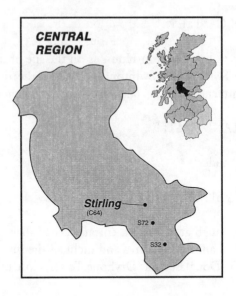

FALKIRK   S32
NS8980

The remains of Falkirk's history have disappeared beneath the
present town. Two battles bear the town's name — the first is
Wallace's 1298 set-piece against Edward I that ended in disaster
for Scotland. The second was the Jacobite victory over the government in 1746. In the churchyard you will find monuments
to some who died in the battles. About two miles south-east of
the town, on a low hill, can be found the Wallace Stone.

TORWOOD CASTLE   S72
NS8384   *Larbert*

An old ruin of obscure history standing in the remains of the
former royal forest of Tor Wood where William Wallace found
shelter after his defeat in the north. Tor Wood was also the place
appointed by King Robert the Bruce as the rendezvous before
the Battle of Bannockburn and from which the Scottish army

moved to take up its chosen position in the wooded New Park, half-a-mile north of the Bannock Burn.

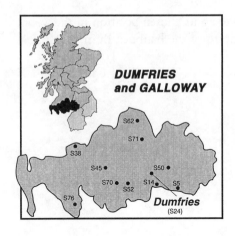

ANNAN CASTLE S5
NY1966 *Annan*

During the turmoil of the Border forays, in 1300 Robert Bruce either built or repaired Annan Castle to be used as a residence. After being crowned at Scone in 1332, Edward Balliol summoned the Scottish nobility to the castle to do him homage. Many skirmishes and battles were recorded over the years and in 1547 an English army captured the town and fired it, thereafter the government levied a sum to be used for repairing the defences. The castle was rebuilt but again demolished in 1570 by an English army. Once more rebuilt it was granted as a place of worship to the impoverished townspeople in 1609. The castle stood on the east bank of the River Annan but there are no remains today.

CAERLAVEROCK CASTLE S14
NY0265 *Dumfries*

> *'I will send you cannon. From Caerlaverock. From*
> *Hermitage, if need be.'*
> WILL IN BLACK DOUGLAS

A formidable fortress standing near the mouth of the River Nith on the Solway shore, the building is one of the finest examples of baronial architecture in Scotland. A square mound to the south of the building marks the site of a previous castle, but the present structure dates from between 1290 and 1300. The triangular shape of the building is unique in Scotland. Ownership of the castle changed many times between the English and Scots and it was involved in much warlike action. In 1312 it was dismantled on the orders of King Robert the Bruce to avoid it being used by the enemy.

The dramatic triangular fortress of Caerlaverock, now surrounded by a beautiful nature reserve

DUMFRIES S24
NX9776

An important military town and base during the Wars of Independence at the eastern entrance to Galloway and the south-west. Look for the sites of the castle and the Grey Friars monastery where Robert the Bruce slew the Red Comyn. No trace now remains of either, other than marker plaques. The ruins of Lincluden College a little further up the River Nith and the not far distant Sweetheart Abbey of Lady Devorgilla fame, a few miles to the south at New Abbey, should be explored.

GLEN TROOL   S38
NX4080   *Newton Stewart*

Towards the southern edge of the Galloway Forest Park lies Glen Trool, scene of the 'Battle of the Steps O'Trool'. Robert the Bruce, with only a small number offollowers, defeated an English force of 2000 men.

KENMURE CASTLE   S45
NX6376   *New Galloway*

The headlong clash was shocking,
explosive, breathtaking.
THE TAPESTRY OF THE BOAR

Now a gutted shell, the fabric dates in its earlier parts from the 16th century. This structure, however, supplanted the previous stronghold of John Balliol that may well have been old at the time of his birth. Said to have been a seat of the Lords of Galloway, his mother was the famed Devorgilla, daughter of the Lord of Galloway and founder of Dulcecorde (better known as Sweetheart) Abbey and Balliol College, Oxford. A later visitor was Mary Queen of Scots. The castle was burned down soon afterwards.

LOCHMABEN CASTLE   S50
NY0881   *Lochmaben*

'Lochmaben and Craig Douglas are smoking ruins.
King James himself made them so.'
WILL IN BLACK DOUGLAS

Granted the territory of Annandale by David I about 1124, the first Bruce tower was built beside Kirk Loch on what is now the golf course. But the ruined Lochmaben Castle on its promontory jutting into the waters of the Castle Loch was a medieval fortress of great strength. Built in the late 1200s, the castle works covered about 16 acres with a fosse or moat filled by water from the loch providing protection. It was seized by Edward I, strengthened and garrisoned and was mostly in English hands. Bestowed by King Robert upon the Earl of Moray, his nephew, it did not return permanently to Scottish hands until 1384. A ghost is said to haunt the place.

MOTE OF URR   S52
NX8164   *Dalbeattie*

This massive earthwork, formerly an island, was a major Norman stronghold with keep, bailey and trenches. The terraces of the medieval town can be sought out on the southern side of the mote.

SANQUHAR CASTLE   S62
NS7809   *Sanquhar*

Little now remains of the castle which stands by the River Nith, south of the town of Sanquhar. Dating from the early 15th century, the castle was owned by the Ross family. In 1630 it was bought by the Duke of Queensberry who also built nearby Drumlanrig.

THREAVE CASTLE   S70
NX7560   *Castle Douglas*

> *'What Lord comes so lightly to Threave?' somebody*
> *demanded, deep-voiced. 'The Lord of Douglas. To pay*
> *respects to the Lady of Galloway.'*
> THE BLACK DOUGLAS IN BLACK DOUGLAS

An island stronghold of the Douglases built by Archibald 'The Grim', 3rd Earl and Lord of Galloway. Now ruined, it is still an impressive 14th century fortress. As the Douglas power was destroyed, it became a royal castle.

TIBBERS CASTLE   S71
NX8698   *Carronbridge*
Slight vestiges of this castle thought to have originated in Roman times remain near to the River Nith and the village of Carronbridge. The castle, rebuilt towards the end of the 13th century was garrisoned by the English, taken by surprise by William Wallace and finally destroyed by Robert the Bruce in 1311.

WHITHORN   S76
NX4440   *Wigtown*
Capital of the Novantes and with a charter from King Robert in 1325, but above all the place in which St Ninian founded the first place of Christian worship in North Britain circa AD450. With the 'Whithorn dig', a museum, and not far away St Ninian's Cave, this is an area worthy of much exploration.

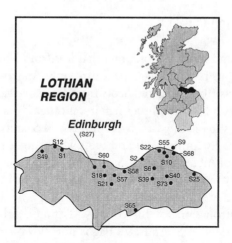

ABERCORN   S1
NT0878   *South Queensferry*

The site of Abercorn Castle lies within the grounds of Hopetoun
House and is close to the village which was the seat of Bishop
Trimuini. The see of Abercorn was established in AD681 and is
one of the earliest Scottish bishoprics.

ABERLADY BAY   S2
NT4580   *Aberlady*

The anchorage grounds in Aberlady bay were until the early 1800s
the port for Haddington, a town of some importance. About a
mile from the village of Aberlady the remains of Luffness Castle
form the basis of Luffness House. Believed to date from the
mid-13th century the castle would seem to have been of some
considerable size with earthworks and moat. Badly damaged
around 1550 the castle has in part survived to this day.

ATHELSTANEFORD   S6
NT5377   *Haddington*

Tradition, and indeed record, says that it is from here that Scotland gained its national flag, the Saltire, or St Andrew's Cross. A force of Picts from Alba and Scots from Dalriada was returning from a raid on Northumbria when it was caught by a host under Athelstane, son of King Athelwolf of the West Saxons. The battle was going badly for the Picts and Scots when Angus mac Fergus, High King of Alba saw a white St Andrew's cross in cloud against the blue sky; and vowing that if the saint would intercede for them with the Almighty and give them victory, he would make Andrew patron saint of his country. Triumph followed with Athelstane slain. A St Andrew's flag is now flown continuously in the village churchyard, above an illustrated plaque of the battle and an information centre is planned.

BASS ROCK   S9
NT6087   *North Berwick*

This impressive island standing in the Firth of Forth off North Berwick is the last in a chain of volcanic masses stretching over the Lothians. Although only one mile in circumference and 350ft high, it appears much larger because of its steep sides and huge form. One of the early Christians of Scotland, St Baldred, had a cell on the island in the early part of the 7th century and it was used as a prison to restrain covenanting ministers during the reign of Charles II. After the death of Claverhouse at the Battle of Killiecrankie and the flight of James VII and II, the rock was captured by the Jacobites and held in the name of the exiled Stuart king for some years. The Bass is a haunt of many seabirds and it has given its name to the Bass Solan Goose.

The massive volcanic rock of Berwick Law

BERWICK LAW   S10
NT5584   *North Berwick*
A mile to the south of North Berwick, this 600ft high volcanic
rockhill provides a major viewpoint for identifying the main
features of the Lothian coast and surrounding plain.

BLACKNESS CASTLE   S12
NT0580   *Linlithgow*
Built in the 14th century on a rocky promontory on the River
Forth the castle was originally a keep. In 1537 it was transformed
into one of Scotland's strongest fortifications. Later used as a
state prison, then a gaol for Covenanters, it became a garrison
and was in use until the early part of this century.

Craigmillar Castle, near Edinburgh, is well worth a visit

CRAIGMILLAR CASTLE
S18
NT2870
See under Edinburgh

DALKEITH CASTLE
S21
NT3367
Dalkeith

> *Morton was not beaten yet, of course; it was not so*
> *easy as that. But he found it expedient to retire to his*
> *own great palace at Dalkeith – the Lion's Den, as it*
> *was called.*
> LORD AND MASTER

The present palace incorporates some remains of the strong castle built originally in the 12th century. A place of siege and bloodshed, it was a stronghold of the Douglas Earls of Morton.

DIRLETON CASTLE

NT5183

S22

North Berwick

The ruins of this impressive castle originally built in the 13th century, stand in a flower garden setting. The old castle was built around a triangular court of the 'cluster donjon' type and additions were made in the 14th and 16th centuries. In 1298 the castle was besieged by Edward I and retaken by the Scots in 1311.

DUNBAR CASTLE

NT6778

S25

Dunbar

*'It was a rash act, was it not, to storm Dunbar
Castle? Rather to invade England without warrant.
There was no need to burn down Wark Castle, the
King of England's own property.'*
JAMIE IN *A FOLLY OF PRINCES*

Believed to have been founded at an early period of the Christian era, the red sandstone ruins of this important stronghold stand on a promontory above Dunbar harbour. The original building was added to and strengthened at different ages after sieges and wars with the English and was burned by the Earl of Shrewsbury in 1548. Mary Queen of Scots and Darnley arrived there after Rizzio's murder in 1566 and she took refuge in the castle after Darnley was blown up at Kirk o'Field, this time with Bothwell.

EDINBURGH

NT2773

S27

*'Swords and arrows and lances are of little avail
against Edinburgh Castle. A thousand men are scarce
worth one cannon.'*
SIR WILL HAY IN *BLACK DOUGLAS*

Exploring Scotland's capital will take you from St Margaret's Chapel at the heart of the ancient castle. Go down the Royal

Mile, which was the spine of the old town, to the Abbey and Palace of Holyroodhouse. Cross the park to Duddingston Loch, once a royal hunting ground, and then on to Craigmillar Castle. Explore the interior of St Giles Cathedral on the High Street and Parliament House, behind the cathedral, now the home of Scotland's supreme courts.

An unusual view of Edinburgh Castle, atop its volcanic rock, showing the old Nor' Loch before it was drained

Continue to Restalrig and Lochend House, the one-time castle of Robert Logan. Merchiston Castle — home of John Napier, the inventor of logarithms — is now a part of Napier University. Other attractions include Greyfriars' Churchyard, John Knox's house and the ancient port of Leith.

The ancient Nether Bow Port seen from the Canongate in the heart of Edinburgh's Old Town

HADDINGTON S39
NT5173
A delightful old county town dating back to the 12th century as a demesne town of the king. Burned down four times, nothing of the early town now remains except the abbey ruins.

HAILES CASTLE   S40
NT5775   *East Linton*

> *'I do not know how this land lies. But — let us pray*
> *that Hailes Castle does not fall, meantime.'*
> ARCHIBALD, MASTER OF DOUGLAS IN A FOLLY OF
> PRINCES

Built in the 13th century near to the village of East Linton by
the Graydon family of Northumberland. Hailes was once of great
dimensions with subsequent rebuilding and extensions added in
the 14th and 16th centuries. A Hepburn possession for most of
its existence, Mary Queen of Scots was seized and brought here
in 1567 by her third husband, James Hepburn, Earl of Bothwell.

LINLITHGOW   S49
NT0077

Here, in what was a busy market town is to be found a remark-
able royal palace. A royal castle of David I, taken by Edward I,
retaken and demolished by Robert the Bruce, it was rebuilt by
David II and expanded. Mary Queen of Scots was born here.
The stunning quadrangle was rebuilt by her son, James VI. Add
to all this a church founded by David I and a nearby battle;
Linlithgow is indeed a place of history, the traditional dowry-
house of Scotland's queens.

NORTH BERWICK   S55
NT5584

Created a Royal Burgh by Robert III, it was a seaport in the time
of Robert II and a place of considerable trade.

Close by the harbour are the remains of the 12th century St
Andrew's Kirk and it was here, in the late 16th century, that a
coven of witches and warlocks are said to have raised the Devil.

PINKIE   S57
NT3472   *Musselburgh*

Close to the A1 road near Musselburgh, the battlefield of Pinkie was the scene of a major disaster for Scotland on the 9th September 1547. The area of the battlefield can be located with ease but there is nothing to mark the site. The English army seized many strongholds in south-east Scotland as a result of this victory.

PRESTONPANS   S58
N3874

> *'Perhaps he will quarter them at Colinton. Or at*
> *Dalkeith. Or at Salt Preston. Since Edinburgh is*
> *so full.'*
> MONTROSE IN *THE YOUNG MONTROSE*

A small town that at one time supplied the whole of eastern Scotland with salt, but is better known for a battle. A victory for Bonnie Prince Charlie, the government General Sir John Cope was the first to reach Coldstream with the news of his defeat. You will find a memorial cairn one mile east of the town.

Restalrig Castle outside Edinburgh had associations with John Napier of Merchiston, inventor of logarithms

RESTALRIG CASTLE S60
NT2874
See under Edinburgh

SOUTRA HOSPITAL S65
NT4558 *Pathhead*
Not far from the summit of Soutra Hill are the last remains of a hospital founded by Malcolm IV in 1164. It is now only an aisle used as a burial vault. The area has been investigated to assist in a study of herbs used in medieval times.

TANTALLON CASTLE S68
NT5985 *North Berwick*

*'He sits secure at Tantallon, and knows that the East
March of the Border is his, and therefore the borderline
with England.'*
WILL IN BLACK DOUGLAS

Once one of the strongest castles in the land with its great curtain wall and massive towers, it cannot fail to impress. Set upon
the cliffs, its base washed on three sides by the sea and guarded
by two ditches of great depth on the landward side, it could only
be entered by the heavily fortified drawbridge. Built sometime
in the 14th century and a stronghold of the Douglas Earls, it was
granted in 1479 to Archibald, fifth Earl of Angus. James V besieged it in 1528 with as many heavy cannon as he could lay his
hands on, but to no avail. Finally in 1651 General Monk dismantled the defences during the Commonwealth occupation.

TRAPRAIN LAW   S73
NT5874   *East Linton*

> *'This south side opens to gentle slopes. They can ride
> out, and up round the skirts to Traprain Law, and so
> make for Lammermuir.'*
> JAMIE IN *A FOLLY OF PRINCES*

This conical hill was named Dunpender and for 300 years or
more was the site of the Celtic township of that name. Before
that time it had been a dwelling place dating back to the Stone
Age. A hoard of silver found here is now in the National Museum of Antiquities, Edinburgh.

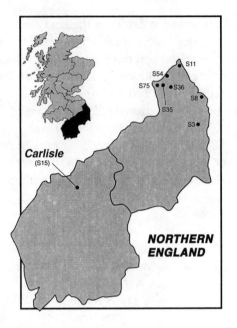

ALNWICK   S3
NU1813

> *'We divide. I take two thousand, and make for*
> *Alnwick, the Percy's town, a dozen miles on.'*
> WILL IN BLACK DOUGLAS

The Northumberland town of the Percys and before them the
De Vescis. The great castle dates from the early 1100s and played
its part in the Anglo-Scots wars. Alnwick also offers Hotspur
Tower, Hulne Priory and Alnwick Abbey, or rather its gatehouse,
to the explorer.

BAMBURGH CASTLE

S8

NU1835   *Bamburgh*

One of the great castles of Northumbria. From the fortress of the Britons and later the royal city of Northumbria until AD954 to the restored Norman castle seen today, Bamburgh has dominated coast and plain in this area of the Borders.

BERWICK-UPON-TWEED

S11

NT9953

'That Stone. Do you still, in your impertinence, say
that is not the Stone of Destiny.'
EDWARD OF ENGLAND IN THE STEPS TO THE EMPTY
THRONE

The most important of the Border towns, Berwick was at one time a royal burgh of Scotland with a powerful castle. The town and castle changed hands many times in medieval days, but now little remains of that period — but there is enough to set the explorer's imagination working. Stand on the road bridge at the railway station and look down to where the trains unload passengers — this was the Great Hall in which Edward I forced Scotland's nobility to sign the Ragman's Roll. Follow the signposted path near the station entrance down to the river and see the Water Tower and the White Wall. Walk the great Elizabethan ramparts and see the older parts of the town which form the living link between the violent history of the wars between England and Scotland and the Union of the Crowns.

CARLISLE

S15

NY3955

...he had no wish, at this stage, to try conclusions with
Harcla, sulking at Carlisle.
THE PRICE OF THE KING'S PEACE

The western English Border fortress town. Dating from the 12th century the great Keep is a grim and gloomy place of immense strength.

The ancient Border fortress town of Carlisle showing the bridge over the Eden with the castle and Cathedral in the background

A city well worth exploring with its cathedral founded in the 13th century and a fortified priory tower. Not far away, close to Brampton, are the ruins of Lanercost Priory with memories of Edward I. This whole area was the western artery for England's armies marching north to war.

FLODDEN
NT9235

S35
Wooler

'*We shall head north by west. Branxton lies west of
Flodden Edge, I know, and Cornhill beyond
Branxton. Tweed cannot be more than six miles. God
with us, we can ford it at Wark or Coldstream.*'
MONTROSE IN *THE CAPTAIN GENERAL*

A great battle between Scotland and England took place here on 9th September 1513. James IV died on this hillside alongside 10,000 of Scotland's fighting men which included 30 of the nobility. Flodden was the last major battle of the longbow. For the explorer this is one of the places to set the imagination racing.

FORD CASTLE   S36
NT9437   *Wooler*

Once an important castle in defence of the English side of the Border, Ford was demolished twice by the Scots. It is now an 18th century restored Gothic castle.

NORHAM CASTLE   S54
NT9047   *Norham*

Once renowned as the most dangerous place in the kingdom of England, Norham is a ruined but nonetheless impressive castle with a massive keep. The first motte and bailey appeared here in 1121 guarding a ford on the River Tweed. The present great stone castle was built in the mid-12th century and some of the stonework of this period remains. Garrisoned strongly for 400 years, the existence of this outstanding castle spans nearly the whole period of the Border wars.

WARK CASTLE   S75
NT8238   *Coldstream*

That day, Wark Castle fell, mined fom beneath.
BLACK DOUGLAS

See under Coldstream

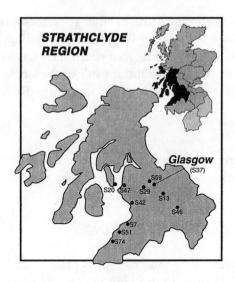

AYR CASTLE
NS3422

S7

Ayr

> *'Your Grace, my Lord Robert. I, Patrick of Dunbar,*
> *humbly crave leave to make my due homage to yourself*
> *a liege Lord.'*
> THE PRICE OF THE KING'S PEACE

The Castle of Ayr was built by William the Lion about 1207, five years before the creation of Ayr into a burgh. The military forces of Edward I of England are assumed to have held possession of the castle during the monarch's seizure of the Lowlands but as it was not large enough for them they built an encampment or temporary barrack which was the scene of a revenge on them by Sir William Wallace. King Robert the Bruce burned the castle in 1298 to prevent it being occupied by the English amy, who were marching westward to attack him. No trace of the castle remains today.

Bothwell Bridge, site of two battles during the seventeenth century

BOTHWELL S13
NS7157

A village which has virtually disappeared in the industrial heart of Lanarkshire. Bridge, church and castle all played their part in Scotland's history. At one time, Bothwell Bridge was the only one over the River Clyde, apart from Glasgow Bridge, and was the site of two battles, in 1650 and 1679; the latter being the more famous one. The oldest part of the church was founded by the Earl of Douglas. Once the main base of the English in the west, the castle was probably the finest in the land and the names of the occupiers read like a roll-call of famous families in the turbulent history of Scotland.

CUMBRAES S20
NS1754 *Largs*

Two islands lying in the Firth of Clyde off the Ayshire coast opposite Largs from which a ferry runs to Millport on Great Cumbrae. It may be possible to identify a likely spot for a Danish camp on Great Cumbrae although no traces remain while on Little Cumbrae are the ruins of a castle used by Robert II, and also the last remnants of a chapel dedicated to St Vey, who is buried nearby.

ELDERSLIE S29
NS4462

The village is reputed to be the birthplace of William Wallace but nothing of that period remains.

GLASGOW S37
NS6373

> *'I am prepared to grant my rescript for the founding of a university college at Glasgow, with all accustomed privileges as at my university of Bologna, under the governance of the good Bishop of Glasgow.'*
> POPE NICHOLAS V IN BLACK DOUGLAS

Unfortunately little remains of Glasgow's historic past. The development of the past 300 years has swept aside the old town. The best place for the explorer to start is beside the River Clyde at the Victoria Bridge. The original settlement was at the ford and later a bridge was built. Bridgegate takes you to Saltmarket, Glasgow Cross and the High Street. Beyond that Castle Street leads to Glasgow Cathedral. With the Trongate (St Thenaus Gate of old), Gallowgate and a number of lesser lanes and closes you have the town and cathedral city of old. Thenau or Thanea was the mother of St Mungo, after whom the cathedral is named.

Glasgow Cathedral – little now, apart from the cathedral, remains of the city's medieval past

IRVINE   S42
NS3239

An ancient royal burgh and important seaport situated at the mouth of the River Garnock. A charter was granted by Robert the Bruce in 1308 to acknowledge the services of the citizens in the wars of the succession. Standing within the burgh is the ruined Seagate Castle which dates from the 16th century and is the site of an earlier stronghold occupied by the Montgomeries of Eglinton. In 1563 Mary Queen of Scots was entertained at the castle by the 3rd Earl, a supporter who fought for her at Langside.

LANARK   S46
NS8843

> 'Hazelrigg?' Wallace jerked. 'I am the Earl of
> Clydesdale' the other rasped. 'Sheriff and...' he got no
> further. 'Then die, murderer!' he was interrupted. 'I
> am Wallace.' And the dirk rose and fell, with savage
> precision.
> THE WALLACE

Famous for its association with Sir William Wallace and a town of great antiquity. A parliament was held here by Kenneth II in AD978 and it became a Royal Burgh in the time of Alexander I. Nothing now remains of the castle and other ancient buildings.

LARGS   S47
NS2059

> *'We must let the enemy come ashore. On the Clyde or*
> *the Cunninghame or the Kyle coasts, if we can get him*
> *there.'*
>
> KING ALEXANDER IN *TRUE THOMAS*

The 2nd of Octber, 1263, is the date which emblazoned the name of the little town of Largs in Scottish history, for it was here that King Haco of Norway had to challenge Alexander III for the sovereignty of the Hebrides and the Isle of Man. The main area of the battle took place along the coast between the ferry pier and the new marina. See the monument to the victory on a small point of land at the southern end.

MAYBOLE   S51
NS2909

Ancient capital of Carrick and stronghold of the Kennedy Earls of Cassillis. Their castle, probably built in the late 16th century, still stands.

RENFREW   S59
NS4966

This industrial and residential town has now almost been absorbed by its bigger neighbour Glasgow. First mentioned in a charter in 1157, the lands and castle were the home of the Stewarts. The battle in which Somerled was killed in 1164 took place in this area.

TURNBERRY CASTLE S74
NS2005 *Girvan*

> *'Hide you there in my castle, Percy. I do not choose to*
> *destroy my own house, where I was born.'*
> ROBERT THE BRUCE IN THE PATH OF THE HERO KING

The remains of this ancient castle, the childhood home of Robert the Bruce, stand on a promontory close to Maidens. Little is known of the origins of the castle but it appears to have been the main seat of the Earls of Carrick. In 1306 it was captured by the English under Earl Percy who held it as a garrison. King Robert stormed it and forced the English to retire to Ayr but the fabric was badly damaged and does not appear to have been repaired or inhabited again.

INDEX